Matrix Warrior

Matrix Warrior

Being the One

Jake Horsley

THOMAS DUNNE BOOKS
ST. MARTIN'S GRIFFIN
NEW YORK

THOMAS DUNNE BOOKS.
An imprint of St. Martin's Press.

www.stmartins.com

ISBN 0-312-32264-X

First published in Great Britain by Gollancz, an imprint of the Orion Publishing Group

First U.S. Edition: November 2003

10 9 8 7 6 5 4 3 2 1

To Mitch Fraas for that red pill.

To the warriors and witches of Atitlan.

To Juan Matus and the Lucid Crew.

And to Lizzie for loving beyond the norm.

Contents

Acknowledgments

First off, my heartfelt thanks and appreciation must go to the Wachowski brothers, Joel Silver, Keanu, Laurence, Carrie-Anne, Hugo, and the cast and crew of *The Matrix* for between them doing such an awesome job of delivering the myth. Without their unparalleled skill and dedication, none of what follows would exist.

Postmortal thanks are extended to Carlos Castaneda and Philip K. Dick for being a constant source of guidance, instruction, and inspiration in the writing of the present work.

To Lyn Birkbeck for pointing me Don Juan–ward when it most counted.

To Simon Spanton at Gollancz for getting this one past the Gatekeepers.

To Vivienne West for sowing the seed, Simeon Every for providing invaluable inspiration in matters of quantum mechanics, and Joseph Kerrick for giving me a handle on the "humaton."

To Tom Dunne and John Parsley for editorial patience and diplomacy in the face of the author-who-would-not-be-censored. And to Mark Fowler for keeping the matrix at arm's length.

And to those readers (you know who you are) who have provided solace in my solipsism and kept me on my toes.

And, of course, to the Universe for always being there.

Energy is the only life and is from the Body, and Reason is the bound or outward circumference of Energy. Energy is Eternal Delight.

What is now proved was once, only imagin'd. Every thing possible to be believed is an image of truth.

The ancient tradition that the world will be consumed in fire at the end of six thousand years is true, as I have heard from Hell. For the cherub with his flaming sword is hereby commanded to leave his guard at the tree of life, and when he does, the whole creation will be consumed, and appear infinite and holy, whereas it now appears finite and corrupt.

If the doors of perception were cleansed everything would appear to man as it is, infinite. For man has closed himself up, till he sees all things thro narrow chinks of his cavern.

Man by his reasoning power can only compare and judge of what he has already perceived. From a perception of only three senses or three elements none could deduce a fourth or fifth. Man's desires are limited by his perceptions, none can desire what he has not perceiv'd.

—William Blake

Matrix Warrior

Preface:
"Not Just a Movie, It's an Experience!"

When the movie *The Matrix* came out in Easter 1999, millions of viewers responded enthusiastically to the state-of-the-art special effects and audacious plotting, and expressed their gratitude for what they perceived—rightly—as a superior piece of Hollywood entertainment. A small handful of viewers, however, persons of unorthodox points of view whose ranks nonetheless appear to be steadily expanding with every passing year, found something in the movie besides a mere *divertissement*. They found a message.

Most of these folk are still in their teens and may have been as young as ten or twelve when they first saw the movie that changed their lives. Many of them probably do too many psychedelics and certainly smoke too much pot, play too many sinister video games, spend too much time alone, and rarely, if ever, read a book. Admittedly, there are plenty of discerning adults who grokked the movie's "message," but the majority of the movie's followers are undoubtedly in their teens and early twenties. A large number of viewers, even if they enjoyed the movie, may have lacked the flexibility and imagination (and perhaps also the disenchantment) necessary to receive the movie at a deeper, all-encompassing level—as "truth." Thousands, maybe millions, of adolescents and teens, however, already predisposed toward the notion that reality is fucked beyond all redemption, embraced *The Matrix* body and soul and swallowed the red pill eagerly, without hesitation or regret. The rest of us, like the movie said, just weren't ready to be unplugged.

The possibility that everything in the movie might be absolutely and totally true, albeit in a disguised and distorted fashion, was a possibility too tantalizing, too satisfying, too damn rebellious and radical for many youngsters to resist. They took the movie on whole, and adapted their *Weltanschauungs* accordingly. *The Matrix*, then, was more than just another sci-fi mind-fuck movie: it was a signal, sent from the real world (the world of Morpheus, Zion, and the *Nebuchadnezzar*) down into this illusory labyrinth world in which we are all ensnared. It was sent in order to alert us to the nature of our predicament, and provide us with the necessary clues by which to get out, while there is still time, and make it back to reality.

Such a belief may not be as deranged as it at first appears, nor necessarily a cause for concern on the part of these kids' parents, already fearing that the gulf between the generations is extending into infinity. These kids may be crazy but they aren't stupid. They know all about myth and legend, even if they don't know Pan from Dionysus or Jung from Joseph Campbell. They know about intellectual exercises, or head games as they call them, and they know that all of this is *metaphor*. They grok instinctively that the message will have lost a great deal of its purity by being filtered down to us through the various media channels—i.e., the matrix—but appreciate that the essence, miraculously, has survived intact. This essence might be reduced to three basic facts or acceptances:

1) This world is a prison, a dream world woven out of our own thoughts, dreams, fears, and desires, in order to blind us to the truth of ourselves.
2) We are slaves. We have no more say in our choices, our lives,

Fig 1: The Red Pill

and our destinies, than does cattle that is herded, or chickens in their coop. We are at the mercy of forces we cannot even begin to comprehend, forces that definitely do not have our welfare at heart.

3) Humanity is a food source, and the world as we know it is simply the elaborate, intricate mechanism by which we are distracted from this fact: that the world is a farm, and we are the livestock. All our dreams then, are dreams of meat, on its way to being eaten.

These are ideas that only the very open-minded or else the extremely disillusioned (or best of all, both) are willing or able to entertain or to assimilate, as having any bearing on reality. As such, they are kept within the comfortable confines of fantasy, be it sci-fi books and movies, ancient mythology, or Hollywood action flicks. And *yet*, these ideas are not actually new.

To varying degrees they are central to systems of human belief extant in most if not all cultures and pertaining throughout all recorded history. For example, that the world is not what it appears to be is something all religions have insisted upon, something that myths have hinted at, and something that science has finally established in this last century, beyond all reasonable (or even unreasonable) doubt.

That we have no actual say in our decisions, that free will is but our fondest and most violently defended illusion, that we are in truth but a minuscule component of some vast mechanism, some greater working which we can barely even imagine from our present perspective; this likewise has been fed to us by religions from childhood to old age. Myths make the same argument implicitly: wherever there is God or gods, all human endeavor is inevitably reduced to ignorant folly; at best it is some sort of divine test, at worst no more than amusement for a cold, indifferent Fate. Worse still, modern science, from Darwinism to chaos theory, has presented the same argument, albeit in rational and not mystical terms, substituting concepts such as gravity and subatomic particles for God or Fate.

However, neither religion nor science has as yet dared to suggest, in anything but passing, that humanity might exist merely to provide sustenance for some other entities of which we are unaware, that prey upon us just as any species preys upon those below it: for survival. Of course, humanity has always considered itself to be the supreme predator in a predatory universe, to be securely placed at the very top of the food chain. True, certain Gnostic texts refer to God Himself as "a maneater," but apart from this rather embarrassing slip (and it is for just such "slips" that the Gnostic texts were excised from the Bible proper), it is only in the realms of ancient myth and, most of all, occult lore, that we find any significant parallels to this last, supremely unpleasant idea. But we will come back to that.

My point for now is merely to show how *The Matrix* brought to a large number of people, in a suitably entertaining, even frivolous and simplistic, fashion, questions that are central to our present predicament as humans, and indeed to the very meaning of what it is to be human. Like all good myths, the movie addresses both individual and universal concerns, real and mundane, and takes them into a more fantastic realm. As a result of their being removed from our everyday frame of reference, these concerns begin to make a new kind of sense to us. The truth dawns, if only for the two hours during which we are transported to an alternate universe, a universe in which nothing is true and, consequently, anything is possible. To put it another way, the frustration, despair, and existential panic; the boredom, anxiety, paranoia, loss of identity, sense of unreality; the feeling of being trapped, of being drained of one's will and energy, of being plotted against, confounded, and blocked at every turn, and above all, the sense of utter meaninglessness and futility that pervades collective and individual life in the twenty-first century, all begin to make perfect sense within the frame of reference provided by *The Matrix*.

This is what myths are all about. They aren't rational explanations of our lives so much as emotional interpretations. They are designed not to explain what's going on, but rather to account for and shed light upon our feelings about what's going on. Myths are collective dreams. So, a myth like *The Matrix*, which suggests that life is a collective dream, is really the ultimate myth-story. It is the myth of humanity itself, a dream within a dream, a myth about a myth, a metaphor for a metaphor. Hence the movie seamlessly fuses science with religion, revealing both to be but alternate, opposing modes of mythology: those of the rational and intuitive modes, or left and right brain respectively. The truth, then, is to be found not through one or the other, but through the correct juxtaposing and balancing of *both*. If life itself is but a temporary, illusory, and even, finally, arbitrary interpretation of energy, then myths are blueprints by which we might come to understand the mental processes that give rise to a given interpretation. It is not that they are outside reality because they are less than it, but on the contrary, they are outside reality because they are the means by which reality is created. In which case a movie, being a hologrammatic package within the greater hologram of life itself, might conceivably be a window, or even a doorway, to that reality which lies beyond. It may just be exactly what the geeks and dopers are trying to tell us it is: Truth.

Like all true myths, *The Matrix* is a journey of individuation, by which the soul, through trial and adversity, purges itself of all that is foreign to it and so comes to experience the totality of itself. This apotheosis of self (in the movie) consists of a form of enlightenment in which the world entire becomes no more than a mirage, a mirage by which the soul is tricked, tested, and challenged. Once Neo is able to "read the code," the game is over; or at least he has moved to the next level. He shakes his head wryly, perhaps a little sadly, and stops the incoming bullets with a lazy wave of his hand, as if to say, "No more of that." By seeing the world as it is he has transformed it from an adversary into an ally, perhaps even a lover: it is subject to his *will*, to shape as he sees fit. This transcendental climax makes *The Matrix*, the most popular (and poetic) action movie ever made, not just a modern myth but a metamyth: a myth about the eternal process by which myths, and humans, are made. It reveals the world itself as a myth, and man as both Messiah and Adversary, still torn between the two opposing sides of his nature.

Since so many adolescent and even older viewers believe the movie to hold secrets that only they can decipher—secrets of empowerment, enlightenment, and emancipation—it would be rash of us to dismiss this possibility without further investigation. If we credit the dopers, movie nerds, and cyberpunks, the carriers of the coming Zeitgeist, with the discernment to tell a simple sci-fi blockbuster from a genuine revelation, then we owe it to them, and to ourselves, to at least entertain the possibility that *The Matrix* is something more than just a movie. Since the kids of today seem to prefer to read from a computer screen; since images, or light, are their chosen medium; since action, fantasy, romance, horror, and special effects are the media by which they interpret life, the universe, and everything; and since religion and science, just as much as ancient mythology, are seen as just part of the conspiracy to trick us into docile obedience and turn us into livestock, "calm as Hindu cows" (as *Fight Club*'s Tyler Durden has it), then the only place *left* to seek meaning is in movies and other popular media. Twenty-five years ago, punk rock gave kids something to believe in and to practice; it served the same or similar purpose as religion would if religion wasn't something that had been forever delegated to the ranks of the damned as "uncool," by these same kids. Today young people become more eclectic with every passing nanosecond, and take their inspiration and guidance wherever they can. Movies are the ultimate art form, and a movie like *The Matrix* combines punk sensibility with philosophical insights, kung fu mysticism, conspiracy theory, occultism, mass destruction chic, psychedelic dream imagery and effects, paranoid awareness, and, last but not least, a messianic message of redemption. As such, it is, for younger generations at least, the holy book of our times. And so I will treat it as exactly that. The following is an *exegesis.*

Maybe the movie is the myth of our time. An ingeniously designed blueprint, a map by which (if followed diligently and relentlessly enough) we may, like Thomas, find the ultimate truth about ourselves. For, as the last great myth of our time (Christianity) had it: "The truth shall make ye free." And freedom is what it's all about. You don't have to be a cyberpunk to know that.

—Jake Horsley, April 2003

First Variable:

Living in a Dream World

i) Reality as a Snare: Postmodernist Twenty-First Century Fragmentation

2003. The millennium has come and gone, leaving Y2K just another failed prophecy, and the end of civilization, postponed again. Yet, in the two and a half years since that monumental letdown, everything has indeed changed.

The collapse of the Twin Towers cancelled forever the collective illusion that some things are built to last, and that any civilization is immune to the backlash of its acts. Human cloning commenced at a public level, forever destroying the fond human conceit of our uniqueness and specialness, while throwing into confusion, maybe even irrelevance, the once central question of "the human soul." (Can souls be cloned along with bodies? Science has refrained from exploring this thorny question.) And last but not least, with the implanting of humans with microchips (starting with children and Alzheimer's patients), the long-awaited fulfilment of the Book of Revelation has finally commenced. Artificial intelligence has at last successfully infiltrated the human organism. Microchip implants, they say, are the investment of the future. Soon everybody will have one, since we won't even exist in a computerized society unless the electronic superstructure can recognize and identify us via this chip. Just as food at the supermarket can't be purchased without getting its bar codes scanned, and just as no one gets back into the dance club without that little black stamp, so no one will buy or sell without their own personal "mark of the beast." Welcome to the millennium.

The microchip has the special distinction of being the first product ever to be advertised in the Bible (chapter 13, verse 17 of Revelation). At long last, God-fearing people everywhere have the opportunity to invest in the Antichrist. Yes, friends, these are peculiar times, times in which it seems as if anyone who *isn't* paranoid may just as well be dead, and probably soon will be. Or as good as.

The assumption of technology to the throne of all human endeavors, its complete and utter centrality and indispensability in our daily lives, is now an accepted fact of twenty-first–century life. We shall term this the externalization process, referring to a worldview in which everything of value is found outside of ourselves. It has also, rather quaintly, been termed materialism. Accordingly, all inner, abstract, or "spiritual" values have been demoted to peripheral and inessential status: they are trimmings or perks, luxuries which we use only for relaxation and entertainment (the same function TV once had, before it became essential to our sanity).

Materialism began to take over our lives completely during the Industrial Revolution, back when people still believed that science and technology were the means to establish a new covenant with God the Father, and to create Heaven on Earth in their lifetimes. By the time the atomic bomb had incinerated several hundred thousand Asian bodies, however, and TVs were turning everyone into zombie consumers, this happy illusion was strictly for flat-earthers and fundamentalists. Realism was taking over. It became clear that technology would never improve the quality of life but only help grease the wheels on our way to species annihilation. That seemed like a valid enough function, however: if we were headed for destruction, let's at least make it as fast and painless as possible.

But humanity is nothing if not gullible, most especially when it comes to believing its own lies. Over time, the spell of technology became so pervasive that people began believing in the Heaven-on-Earth model again (even if, by now, God the Father had definitely been removed from the picture). The sheer power and scope of our machines was so intoxicating that we once again began to believe (just as H.G. Wells and the utopians had believed) that we could literally accomplish anything. If the planet is being destroyed, that's okay. We'll just move to another one. If society is being overrun by crime and insanity, that's okay too. We'll just build bigger, better prisons and figure out which gene is responsible. Or if that fails, we'll just restructure society and make it one *big* prison, and make sure all the defectives are tagged and marked with microchip implants to keep them in line, while the law-abiding citizens can abide by the law and walk the line. Even if death threatens, as it must, to spoil all our fondest plans for the future, there's still a solution! Immortality pills, organ transplants, human cloning, transference of consciousness to computer drives. Death is no longer a downer for the men who would be gods.

The laws of nature were made, like all rules, to be broken. Man, the scientist, the rational being determined to improve on all the parts of existence he found personally inconvenient, was, as Mary Shelley put it, "the modern Prometheus." And Prometheus is another name, in another, darker myth, for Lucifer.

So now we live in postmillennial, postmodernist times. We live in a consumer culture in which everything that exists outside of ourselves is there to be either hunted, killed, bagged, shelved, bought, sold, reformed, consumed, seduced, or if necessary, destroyed completely. The world is our oyster, and it exists solely to be cracked open by force and devoured, preferably in one big, messy gulp. If it turns out there was a pearl in the shell, then we may never even know. Or possibly only in the moment when we choke on it.

The desire to dominate and control our environment is a desire that humans alone of all the animals possess. It is at base a schizophrenic desire, since it assumes a separation between ourselves and our environment. The Earth created humans and all other living creatures, presumably for its own good reasons, but it is humans who made the world. And since the world as we have made it is at odds with the environment, then humanity has been forced to choose where to pledge its allegiance. By the evidence at hand, it has chosen the world—possibly out of a mixture of pride and ingratitude—and to all appearances, it has made the wrong choice. But who are we to judge? The catch in this choice is that the world which we have created, having no corresponding reality within ourselves—no organic vitality or substance as such—cannot physically sustain us. The longer we remain plugged into this world, the more deeply immersed in it we become, the further from our natural environment and our biological nature we stray, the more at odds with it we are, the more schizophrenic we grow, the weaker, more desperate and alienated our lives become. Hence, what we have called the postmodernist consumer society is a psychotic dream world in which the human spirit and body have trapped themselves. And we have become unwittingly enslaved to the dark, destructive agenda of this world. Exactly as in *The Matrix!*

Once again, the crux of the error here, the nature of this rebellion, and the essence of our damnation or fall from grace (if such they are), lie in the strange capacity of humans to project their desires, hopes, fears, and beliefs *outward*, to seek meaning outside of themselves rather than in the only place where meaning might logically be found—within. By neglecting and denying the inner processes of the psyche and soul, and focusing exclusively on the outer achievements of mind and body, we have effectively stripped existence of all meaning, purpose, value, and yes, reality.

Native Americans (and shamans from all cultures) have a particular view of reality that may be pertinent here. First off, they are animists, which is to say they believe that all of nature, from the lowest grub or pebble all the way to the most distant star, is imbued with life, with consciousness. They believe it is possible to communicate and interact with this life or consciousness, via the medium of spirits residing inside every molecule of physical matter. Through communication, they might thereby discover the true nature and purpose of existence. To them, all life is one life, a New Age platitude that nonetheless has a most practical application.

Animism posits a universe that is a living organism, making all beings that exist within this universe parts of that organism—just as the cells and organs of the human body exist within it—separate and individual (and even conscious) entities, and yet obviously wholly dependent upon and subservient to the greater body. To the animistic Native Americans, Mother Nature is a matrix, but a matrix that nurtures and sustains us like a womb, until, at a given point, when we are ready, it gives birth to us. Shamanically speaking, this is the birth of the Spirit, often coinciding with the moment of physical death. To Christians, it is the Resurrection.

The second point I want to mention is the Native American belief that all technology, even the good kind, has a debilitating effect on the spirit of man. Take the simple example of an electric heater. Very convenient, seemingly indispensable on a cold evening, if we are not to be condemned to a restless night of shivering, stamping our feet, and rubbing our hands together, cursing the

Fig 2: Technological matrix vs. organic matrix

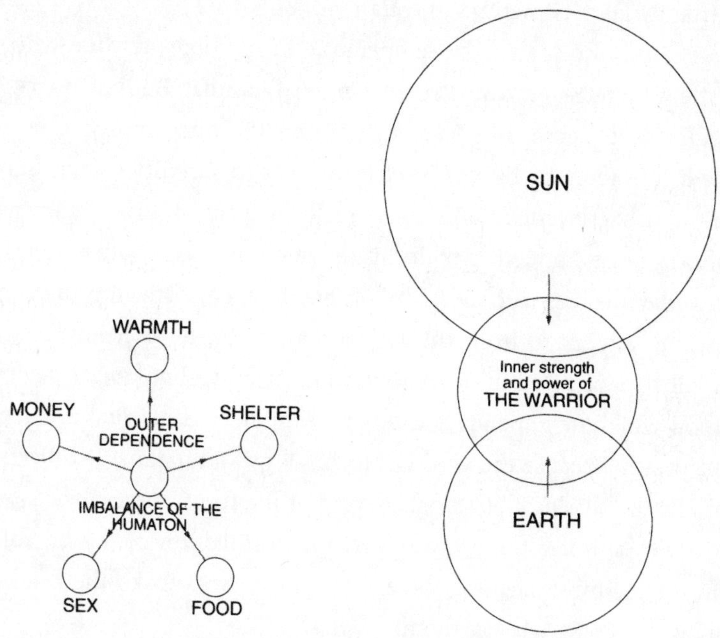

ruthless power of the elements. Yet for the Native American, and indeed for the warrior of any caste or creed, the elements are there to test and prove him, to force him to grow in stamina and resilience, and to develop his inner resources: A warrior faced with a night in the cold and no heater must use his wits, and above all, his *will* (see Glossary), in order to turn the situation to his favor. Maybe he smashes a chair and builds a well-contained fire in the corner. Or maybe, like Han Solo saving Luke in *The Empire Strikes Back*, he cuts open a large biped and takes shelter in its entrails. At worst, the warrior must stand his ground and face the cold without fear, bitterness, or regret. He must give in to it and allow it to teach him. He may listen to his body's internal responses and, if sufficiently detached and resourceful, he may summon the necessary heat from within his body to counter the cold without. If all else fails, he will certainly learn something through failing.

The mind can alter the temperature of the body; anyone who's suffered intense embarrassment can testify to that. But our warrior might never learn this—never even have the opportunity to consider it—while he has his electrical heater to simplify things. Certainly, it's convenient. But is it really helpful? Native American belief goes even further than this, however. Just as a Native American may decline to have his photograph taken, believing that, by making an image from the light of his body, he is losing some small part of his soul, so it follows that any technological device upon which he depends is subtly robbing him of his vital essence, his power. Because the world of technology and manmade objects, unlike the world of Nature, is devoid of life force, these objects, in order to animate themselves (perhaps in imitation of the organic universe), must *steal* life force from those who make them and, above all, those who *use* them.

A musician knows this intuitively: he puts his soul into his instrument until it becomes a part of him. A warrior knows that this is true of everything we touch, and that the manner in which we touch and use the items of our lives, how we think and feel about them, determines the kind of spirit with which we imbue them. And he knows that eventually, once enough power has been transferred to them, for good or for evil, these objects will become living things.

Most of the world as made by humans is a fairly ugly and ungainly affair. It lives but it does not know why. Like Shelley's creature, it has been built for all the wrong reasons, then cruelly rejected, or at best mistreated, out of shame that it did not turn out as we had hoped it would. And so it turns against us. The organic matrix of shamans and sorcerers is a reality (that is, an interpretation) full of mystery, power, and magic. It is a world built consciously, as an act of love and will. As such it is a garden of earthly (and unearthly) delights and offers perhaps an infinite variety of pleasures to those who live within it.

The mechanical matrix of postmodern consumer society, built by ordinary men and women, is a reality that is indeed a snare, serving only to isolate its inhabitants from a truer, wider, and richer interpretation in which all things are interwoven and cooperative. The matrix we live in, and which we uphold with each and every one of our thoughts (though as we shall see, these thoughts are not our own), is a world built blindly, through fear and rationality, a prison pervaded by misery, hostility, confusion, resentment, and despair. It ain't no playground. And if it's a game, then it's one which few of us ever get to enjoy playing—perhaps because no one ever told us the rules.

ii) We Are Not Amused: Rules for Beginners

First rule: Plugged-in humans are defined above all by externals

Be transparent. Make sure your goals are common goals that all others share. Ensure your opinions are not your own but come from other people. This way you may avoid confusing people. By the same token, it is preferable never to say what you mean. Also, try not to mean what you say. Genuineness is considered to be threatening within polite matrix society. Therefore, a functional but rigid and unchanging façade is essential to good relations.

Second rule: You are what you own

Plugged-in humans are collectors. The more objects you can acquire, the higher your status will become in other people's eyes. Most especially if they are useless objects. Possessions are extensions of the personality, ergo the more accessories you can gather, the larger and more complex your personality becomes. Above all, black shiny objects, such as sleek designer shades and swishy cell phones, serve to augment individual cool. It is important to remember, however, that these items are not meant to obscure the personality, but rather to replace it entirely with an effectively shallow façade. With enough accessories in your BMW, who cares if it doesn't run so good, or how much gas it consumes?

Third rule: What people say and think about you is all-important

The primary motivation of all matrix-aligned humans is *to be liked*. The more people who like you, and the more those people like you, the more important you become to them, and so to yourself. Since plugged-in humans don't like what they don't understand, it

Fig 3: Life in the matrix for the humaton

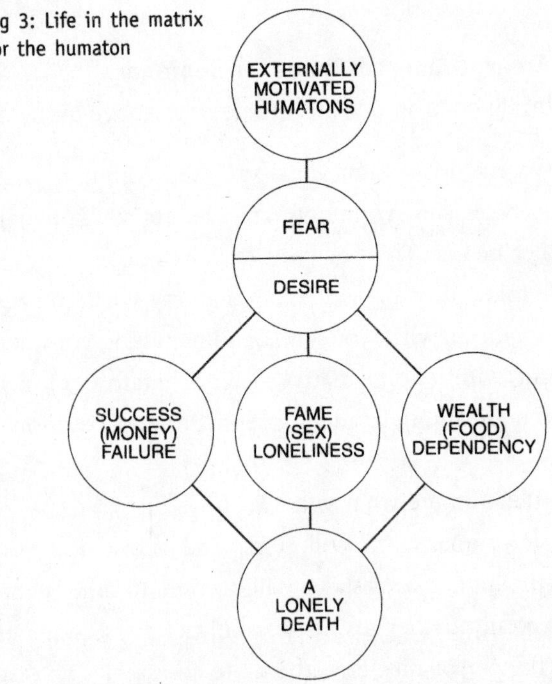

is essential to be straightforward, simple, predictable, and to avoid unusual acts or original thoughts whenever possible. Since plugged-in humans have little or no interest or concern besides themselves, it is important also never to infringe overly on such a person's "space." In conversation, avoid eye contact that lasts for more than a moment. Any direct or personal questions should be kept to a minimum, and generally reserved for extreme circumstances, i.e., when it would be impolite not to ask them. Listening is not mandatory. Plugged-in humans do not as a general rule listen, but rather await their turn to speak. Therefore it is only polite to do the same, and to refrain whenever possible from paying too close attention to the other person's feelings or needs, since this will only make them self-conscious.

Fourth rule: Extreme emotions should be repressed

Plugged-in people, since their primary concern is to be liked, endeavor to maintain an appearance of mildness, consideration, and civility at all times. Any acts or words that might cause offense must be scrupulously avoided. Plugged-in people are easily offended, for they are extremely sensitive to their own feelings; in fact, this is all they think about. Hence, one must maintain a healthy façade of politeness at all times—until, that is, one's own feelings have in some way been affronted. Under such conditions, direct confrontation is to be avoided whenever possible since this would entail emotional engagement with the other, and as such cause discomfort to both parties. Anger should be repressed and rechanneled into more subtle, covert, and petty acts, so that the offending party may never become fully aware of having offended; instead he or she will dimly sense that something is amiss in the relationship, and so be tormented by guilt and uncertainty. Plugged-in people rarely allow themselves to experience strong emotions, such as rage or grief, and if they do, they invariably ensure that its expression is indirect, and convenient, for example, with complete strangers or in wildly inappropriate circumstances. This way they can emote without revealing anything or in any way compromising themselves. Indignation, resentment, bitterness, arrogance, self-pity, contempt, and a thinly veiled hostility are the preferred emotional responses of plugged-in people, and the marks of true character within the social matrix.

Fifth rule: Plugged-in people always compare themselves to others

Every individual is special and unique, and as such, more important than everyone else. It is the single agenda of every separate entity to aggrandize itself in any way possible. The means of this self-aggrandizement center around comparing oneself to others, to one's advantage wherever possible. The more one can belittle others and make them feel inferior, the more superior one may thereby become in their eyes, and hence in one's own. The matrix social arena is based on the interplay of egos, all of which are vying for power over all others. For matrix-aligned humans, all self-esteem revolves around external accomplishment, acquisitions, and the accolades of one's fellow humans. Existence is by nature competitive. All power, as such, depends upon control and mastery, not over the self but over others. The more power one can steal from others, the more one has for oneself.

Conversely, the more empowered others become in relation to oneself, the less power one has over them. This is because egos define themselves through comparison with others and through external factors rather than through any inner sense of value or worth. The ego *competes* with other egos, knowing that only the best ego will win, and that winner takes all. As such, the plugged-in human is by nature set against all other humans in a fight for survival, not of the physical being but of the *ego*. Therefore, innate but carefully concealed hostility is the most constant modality of humans functioning within the social matrix.

Sixth rule: Within the matrix, fame is the Holy Grail of all personal aspiration

The ultimate goal of plugged-in people is threefold: success, wealth, and fame. The rationale behind these goals is single, however. Together they reap the maximum amount of power over other humans. By placing oneself in the highest regard of the greatest number of people, one thereby steals the optimum amount of power from them. Fame is the ultimate goal of all plugged-in people (even if only a handful ever attain it), since it presupposes the other two. Fame ensures both wealth and success but takes things to the next level, that of true power. By achieving the adoration and envy of the world simply by being wealthy and successful, one is secure in the knowledge of one's superiority: millions of people adore one, and yet are secretly despised for it. Hence one's power over them is complete, and the ego becomes, at long last, supreme, the god of its own world. For most plugged-in humans, however, this is something that can only ever be enjoyed vicariously.

Seventh rule: Plugged-in humans need someone to worship and someone to debase

In order for the collective's envy of a given, privileged individual (Keanu Reeves, for example) not to spoil the pleasure they get from adoring him, it is important to foster and maintain the delusion that, some day, they will attain similar or even greater glory themselves. The nature of the plugged-in human is to worship what he reviles and revile what he worships. For at the base of all his acts is a sense of self-loathing and unworthiness. Plugged-in humans look up to those humans to whom they feel inferior, and take gratification from this act of worship. On the other hand, they look down upon those humans whom they perceive as inferior to them, and likewise find fulfilment in this act of debasement. And all the while they take pride in their belief that "all men are created equal."

iii) The Seven Deadly Virtues: Primary Motivating Factors for Plugged-in Humans

Greed

As Gordon Gekko assured us, "greed is good." Greed is the impulse toward the accumulation of property, be it money, food, sexual partners, knowledge, or power. Since greed implies excess (i.e., can only be satisfied by having more than one needs), the nature of such compulsive acquisition is to covet things which one does not really want, or have any use for. And since the rationale behind greed (what makes it good) is that by acquiring things we can favorably compare ourselves to others, who have fewer things, greed is most fully vindicated when we are able to acquire not only what we don't need, but what others palpably do need, and quite badly, but cannot have (partly because we have taken it for ourselves). Greed is industry. It empowers, and inspires the individual to perform at a peak capacity, even if he must kill himself in the process (and cause everyone else to starve). Greed is especially effective for keeping plugged-in humans plugged in because it is wholly outer-directed. The greater one's spiritual emptiness, the stronger the need to fill one's life with material goodies. Thus, the matrix perpetuates itself indefinitely.

Lust

The desire for sexual satisfaction is also primary to plugged-in humans. It is not a hormonal desire, however, since plugged-in humans, by becoming part of the greater mechanism of the matrix, have evolved beyond their animal physicality and are no longer organic beings. They are driven not by biological but by psychological/emotional needs. Hence, the desire for sex, once healthy and natural, has become, like all fake virtues, the desire of the ego for self-aggrandizement (often masquerading as self-debasement). The more people one can fuck, the more self-esteem the ego may gather; the stronger it becomes, the more power it perceives itself to have over others. Sexual gratification, therefore, must always include some element of contempt and even debasement of the other, in order to ensure that there is no possibility of real connection. Such connection is fatal to a plugged-in human, since empathy always entails a loss of self and a corresponding weakening of the ego, which thrives on isolation. Hence, to plugged-in humans the lust mechanism is unrelated to any true sexual desire for union, and relates rather to the need to dominate.

Ambition

Closely related to greed, ambition is the preprogrammed desire, present in all plugged-in humans, to serve the system to fullest capacity, and so reap the favor and benefit of the system, or matrix. Once again, ambition must always be externally directed. Success cannot be measured in terms of any inner sense of well-being, but only according to external assurances from others that, indeed, one is a success. If the inner voice of a plugged-in human (insofar as he or she still has an inner voice) tells them that their success is somehow unsatisfying or meaningless to them, it is expedient that this voice of doubt be drowned out at once by a sensory overload of external stimuli. These stimuli (fellow plugged-in humans) will duly reassure us that, yes, this is success, and of course, we must feel good about it. In time, the fully adapted matrix human learns to measure his or her worth entirely by social criteria, i.e., what others say. Since the matrix tells us we are successful, and that we must feel good about it, then it must be true. At which point, any friends or acquaintances who do not support us in this view, or who dare to question the value of our ambitions, must be ruthlessly removed from our social circles. Ambition is fulfilled through service to the whole—in this case, the social matrix which tells us what to desire and how, precisely, to get it.

Envy

Envy is the means by which the ego aspires to what it is not. It is envy for the neighbor's Porsche or the best friend's girl that fires a plugged-in human's greed, lust, and ambition, and allows it to become a driving force in life. Since the egos of all plugged-in humans are intrinsically unstable, insecure, and racked by doubt and self-loathing, it is only natural for them to wish to be everything that they are not. Envy also keeps the plugged-in humans' resentment and hostility towards others alive and bristling, giving their acts and words the necessary edge to cut through the competition. As we saw in rule seven, plugged-in humans invariably despise those they admire (which is why falling in love is total anathema to plugged-in humans, though they talk about it almost constantly), and this conflicting emotion is reconciled in the fake virtue of envy. All superior egos serve to remind the inferior ego of its own worthlessness. This in turn gives the ego impetus, through subterfuge and deceit, to buy, beg, or steal, whatever it needs to become equal to other egos, and eventually to surpass them altogether.

Conceit and Self-Pity

Once known as pride, the plugged-in human has replaced such a noble sin with the more comfortable (fake) virtue of conceit. Since pride implies a self-awareness and appreciation of one's virtues, strengths, and deeds—and since such awareness is not available to plugged-in humans due to their complete refusal to examine their lives—the only means for the plugged-in human to appreciate himself is to compare himself to others and decide, on all occasions, that he is more important than everyone else. Conceit is the ability to value one's own feelings, ideas, opinions, and decisions as infinitely superior to everyone else's, even when they are quite obviously nothing of the kind (even, in fact, when they are not one's own at all, but stolen or borrowed from others). Conceit is the ability, central to the makeup of all plugged-in humans, to think exclusively and constantly about the self, to take one's own experiences, be they in the nature of blessing or curse, with utmost seriousness and to regard those of everyone else with a sneering indifference or at best, a supercilious pity.

Conceit is really self-pity masquerading as self-importance, however. It is the means by which plugged-in humans hide, from themselves and others, the insidious, crippling fact of their own self-loathing. Hence it is perhaps the most valuable of all fake virtues within the social matrix. Plugged-in humans love nothing more than to feel sorry for themselves, to feed their sense of being better than their circumstances, without ever taking responsibility for having created these circumstances in the first place. Thus it is that self-pity masquerades as self-importance, and conceit acts as a cover for self-loathing.

Indignation

As mentioned in rule four, plugged-in humans work hard at keeping their true feelings under wraps. This is because strong emotions, even negative ones such as sorrow or wrath, have the undesirable effect of causing the ego to shift and transform under duress. Since the small, tight, fixed ego is the central possession of all plugged-in humans (it is in fact the plug-in point itself, the nodule that hardwires them to the matrix), it is essential to select for expression only those emotions that allow the ego to remain fixed in its familiar position and modality. Because the basic modality of the plugged-in human is one of hostility and contempt toward all others, the most effective emotion (one that allows this hostility and contempt to express itself in the most righteous manner) is that of indignation. Plugged-in humans tend to spend most of their lives in a state of indignation, and the matrix plays upon this. Public phones with coins jammed in them, buses that come in threes after a half-hour wait, CD wrappers that are almost impossible to open, switchboard systems that take an obscene amount of time and concentration to penetrate—all these things are deliberately designed and maintained by the matrix, and the humans working within it, to create the maximum amount of indignation. Indignation also relates to conceit: the more conceited one is, the more indignation one may indulge in; the more indignation, the more conceited one becomes.

Sloth

All plugged-in humans are naturally apathetic, indolent, and lazy. The matrix encourages ambition, social climbing, and all external goals or material industry; but it strongly discourages anything resembling real effort, will, or discipline. This is why outer goals are stressed so insistently, since it is possible to attain fame and wealth without ever having to develop one's character or inner nature. Above all, it is essential to maintain the proper degree of complacency, the smug self-satisfaction common to all plugged-in humans, and not to bid for any real, lasting change. Constant stagnation is the basis of the matrix; without this it could not exist.

Such stagnation depends upon fostering the illusion of change in order to distract plugged-in humans from the rank and putrid truth of their lives.

Hence, it is mandatory that plugged-in humans continue to allow themselves to be distracted by constant stimuli, those of external goals, desires, problems, fears, and so forth (be they relating to food, shelter, sex, money, fame, or power). In this way, plugged-in humans continue to neglect utterly their inner needs and remain in a state of constant stagnation. Thus, while plugged-in humans are physically and materially active, in constant struggle to overcome material obstacles and solve mundane problems, they are entirely passive at an inner or spiritual level, to the point where the muscles of the creative imagination (the one thing the matrix truly fears) have atrophied and barely work at all, save in a few, rare individuals.

In summation, all plugged-in humans (which is to say, just about everyone everywhere, although western civilized folk have the edge) are playing the game of consensus reality whether they are aware of it or not, and are playing by rules which they neither invented nor ever consciously agreed to. In most cases, in fact, they are grossly unaware that such rules even exist. (Of course, the laws of physics, of entropy, disease, death, sexuality, and so forth, are also rules which we never agreed to; but they go a lot deeper, and we shall get to them later.) And oddly enough, the matrix of consensus reality has been set up in such a way that it is necessary to first understand the rules before you can begin changing, bending, or breaking them. So this is an option of which the vast majority of plugged-in humans never become aware. The first step to freedom, logically, is admitting that you are a slave. This is not an easy step for most plugged-in humans to take.

The fact that many plugged-in humans believe in both God *and* Satan, in Fate and "free will," without ever becoming aware of the glaring contradiction in such a belief system, lets us know just how deep the denial goes. Logically, either God runs the world, or Satan does. It can't be both. Either our actions are mapped out in advance by some force we call "Fate," or we ourselves decide each and every moment, using some faculty called "will." There is however a third option, and this is that God and Satan work together in some mysterious manner, that Satan is just a prison guard, a prison guard who keeps us from getting to God until we have proved ourselves smart enough to get by him; in which case, "free will" is something only a very few individuals ever attain. It's the prize for those precious, Lucid few (see Glossary) who have dared to sneak past the prison guard and escape a wholly unacceptable fate. Here is where the matrix warrior comes in.

iv) Automatons 'R' Us

All the way back in the 1940s, Jose Delgado developed a means to electronically control a bull by implanting it with a miniature transmitter that sent a microwave signal to the bull's brain and stopped it in the middle of its charge. Recently, there have been reports of radio-controlled rats, similarly implanted with the dreaded microchip, being sent into burning buildings to locate any inhabitants still inside. (What they do when they find these people is less clear; presumably the rats are equipped with minicams and radio back their location to the firefighters.) Since criminals and children (and Alzheimer's patients) are already being implanted with the same or similar devices, then radio-controlled humans may be just around the next corner. Or perhaps these organic robots are already walking among us? Yet essentially, such developments are really only the latest stage—the culmination—of a process that has been underway ever since humans developed their very first technology, a rational system of communication.

If humanity is a single organism with—at present, and still counting—six billion parts, then the consciousness of this organism must be parceled out accordingly to each and every one of these parts. Equally, since everything that can be measured is finite, we may presume there to be a finite amount of thought energy (human consciousness) that is being distributed among the various vessels that we know of as individual humans. Before the inception of structured language, unless we were simply grunting primates (and there is plenty of evidence to refute this), it seems likely that the human race–organism was once fully aware of the interconnectedness of its parts; that it was, in fact, like any other organism, in constant communication with itself. This implies a kind of nomadic, tribal, telepathic society, roaming the Earth, hunting and gathering, and propagating the species. Such a species-organism would be wholly connected to the Earth in a way that we cannot even imagine today, safe and sound as we are in our metallic shells and brick-and-mortar boxes.

Today, we are six billion strong, and completely disconnected from the Earth and from one another. And yet our basic need to exist within some greater matrix persists, and may even be primary to our survival. To this end, we have created a matrix all our own, in a perhaps vain, certainly perverse imitation of the organic matrix to which we once so happily belonged. Primal consciousness, transmitted through DNA (adhering to Sheldrake's theory of morphic resonance), can be shared by all members of a given species in some mysterious fashion that allows all the "parts" to retain their individuality while still belonging to a greater whole. Every species is a sort of hive, connected by some tenuous and invisible thread, some "strange attractor" or blueprint. It is this genealogy that keeps all the parts in constant communication even though they may never physically meet. This is how instincts develop: whatever one member of a species learns is passed on to all the others, by osmosis if you will, via their DNA. (So, if enough monkeys on one island figure out how to scrub and eat potatoes, eventually all the monkeys on all the other islands will also be doing it. And without so much as a single telegram.)

Exclusively rational consciousness, on the other hand, which so far only humans have been fool enough to develop, is an altogether different affair. Since it depends on thought and not on feelings, it is by nature compartmentalized. Rationality is what measures energy or awareness out into separate units. What rations or measures, however, also limits and confines. Feeling may just be infinite, but thought (at least thought based on structured language, i.e., packages of information, no matter how many of them) is inevitably limited to a set number of units. Every rational being is like a highly advanced computer with a finite number of options to its program. Like the Terminator in the movie of the same name, for any given circumstance we have a set number of possible responses; all we do is choose from these set responses. So-called free will, therefore, is *impossible for a rational being.*

What happens when rational left-brain consciousness is shared is the opposite of what happens when intuitive right-brain consciousness is shared: the species becomes fragmented, disconnected, and, paradoxically, each of the separate parts loses all semblance of individuality. Since species members all partake of the same matrix, and yet are isolated within it by their own thought processes (rational thought being *separative* thought), what we get is a species that is, in a sense, trapped by its own thoughts. Such a matrix is non-sustaining, and the species or individual that exists within it, since it lacks the organic connection to sustain it, gets ever busier building external devices to compensate for its lack of connectivity, devices that only serve to isolate it further. Since these devices merely consolidate the sense of separation by allowing individuals to disconnect more and more from the collective species consciousness, the technological, rational matrix becomes smaller, more confining, and more oppressive, even as it becomes more complex and elaborate.

Such a matrix eventually takes over not only the acts but even the thoughts and feelings of everyone in it; in imitation of the true organic matrix, it begins to program its inhabitants with "instincts" and behavioral patterns, and, after a time, these become inescapable. This matrix downloads its "reality" straight into the species' DNA, and thence into our emotions and thoughts. So the latest advance of microchip transmitter-receivers, by which the human organism becomes a kind of accessory to the machine, plugged into a computer superstructure (termed AI in the movie), is, as I say, merely the culmination of a process that began a long, long time ago. We are already hardwired to the main drive. We are *automatons.*

It's not merely that we buy what we are told to buy, cross over when told to cross, and vote for whomever we're told to vote for; we think and feel only and exactly what we have been programmed to think and feel by the social matrix into which we were inserted at birth. And from the moment of birth, every single person we encounter is there to shape and mold our interpretation of reality until we "fit." They are, from Mom and Pop on down, our programmers. Their primary function is to turn us into efficient and homogeneous units within the life-support system of this, our brave new machine world.

In the twenty-first century, technology has taken this programming process to a state-of-the-art efficiency and ease. One-year-olds are plopped down in front of the TV screen so Mom can take a breather. Six-year-olds are given cell phones so they can call Pop when school's out. Ten-year-olds are given computers in their rooms to do their homework and to play simulation games. And kids are now being "tagged" with sensor transmitter microchips, inserted permanently into their bodies, just in case they ever get lost or kidnapped. The recent, highly publicized kidnapping and murder of two prepubescent girls in Soham, England, has now opened the public mind and body to the implant. Brave new world indeed. By the time we are adolescents we are fully plugged in, and yet we probably don't even know a zebra from a gazelle (unless we happen to have seen them on TV).

Morpheus asks Neo, "What is real?" He answers his own question, convincingly, by explaining how our experience of reality is handed down to us by the senses, via electrical signals to the brain. In which case, he argues, what is to stop the brain from being tricked into *believing* it is experiencing something, when all that is really happening is that it is being bombarded with electrical signals?

Where once the human organism allowed itself to be sustained, nurtured, and informed by the natural stimuli of earth, wind, sun, and rain, now it is cocooned, confined, and molded by electronic stimuli, the sources of which are almost wholly artificial. We are no longer organisms. We are mechanisms.

You too could be the One!

It is helpful to remember, whenever despair threatens to overwhelm us at the apparent inescapability of our fate, that even Neo himself was once just another helpless automaton, plugged into an evil regime with nothing besides a splinter in his brain to distinguish him from the flock and lead him through the darkness.

When we first meet Thomas Anderson, he is sleeping at his computer, a cyber nerd with no life to speak of beyond his console. He awakes to see a message coming from nowhere on the screen, coming in fact from his Anima, Trinity, tweaking his curiosity and desire. He is told to "follow the white rabbit," i.e., pursue an organic, illogical, perhaps even magical, train of thought, wherever it may lead him. Then comes "knock knock." By this point, doubting Thomas does not need to ask "Who's there?" He already knows.

Trinity, Morpheus, and the *Nebuchadnezzar* team are all operating both inside and outside the matrix within which Thomas is trapped. They are able to hack into "reality" (as Thomas still believes it to be), for the simple reason that they have discovered that it is nothing of the kind but only a simulation, a rational, artificial interpretation of life. As such, they don't need to be bound by its laws, although they can still operate within it. At this point, Thomas has no inkling (besides that splinter) of the way things really are. He doesn't know what the matrix is, only that it is "out there," somewhere, and that it has him. The closest he gets to it for now is when he asks his acidhead client, "Ever have the feeling you're not sure if you're awake or still dreaming?" The acidhead puts it down to mescaline and invites Thomas along to a party. Thomas, anything but a socialite, is about to decline when he spots the white rabbit tattoo on the acid chick's shoulder, and agrees to go. Just like Alice, he is drawn by curiosity, and perhaps also boredom. He is learning to spot and read and follow the signs. The matrix is beginning to talk to him, albeit through the intervention of Trinity.

At the club Thomas meets Trinity and she whispers seductively in his ear, telling him that she knows "why [he] can't sleep at night." Trinity knows everything there is to know about Thomas/Neo. She knows because, if Morpheus and his crew can hack into the matrix, then presumably they can also watch any part of it they need to. From their point of view, it's like a vast movie archive of human experiences. In which case, they would certainly have gone over Thomas's life with great precision, in order to be sure that he is "the One." Beyond this, they would have wanted to find out what sort of person he is, what his weaknesses are, his strengths, his dreams, his nightmares. Not only that, but they can probably even see Thomas's entire "future life" too, the fate which the matrix (by tapping into his sleeping mind) has already designed for him. Of course Thomas will escape this fate, and so his future life will never come to pass, just as his past will cease to exist, as if it had never happened. So everything Thomas has come to believe about himself, everything he believes himself to be, is a lie. It's fake. "The matrix cannot tell you who you are," Trinity tells Neo on his trip to the Oracle. It can only tell him what he might have been.

Since the matrix is designed to enslave and not to empower, whatever "self" or identity or destiny it creates for us is bound to be an ultimately confining, restrictive, and paltry one. At the start of the movie, Thomas is listless, despondent, fuzzy, pale, and slightly bewildered. He lives alone and seems driven, if driven at all, by an intense desire to answer some vague question which he presumably does not even fully understand. Beyond that, he seems lifeless, indolent, as if having given in to a mundane and dreary fate which he never wished for, but cannot escape or improve upon. At his place of work, while window cleaners wipe the glass (despite itself, the matrix is hinting at the need for lucidity?), Thomas's superior tells him that he has "a problem with authority," and believes "the rules do not apply" to him. Obviously, Thomas is mistaken. He is "part of a whole," just another component in the machine. In a few moments, with the intervention of Morpheus and of the matrix itself, in the form of two sinister Gatekeepers (see

Glossary), Thomas will prove to his superior just how different he is. Thomas has a hidden side, an alter ego, and is wanted by just about everybody.

It is when Thomas receives the package with the cell phone inside, or rather at the moment when the phone rings, that his old life effectively ends. The spell is broken. Until this moment, Thomas's life has been no more than a fuzzy, forgettable dream, a bad mescaline trip. His every "act" within this dream world has been predetermined, programmed from without by a vast, invisible circuit board. This corporate brain has fed him every last one of his thoughts, emotions, and responses, and kept him in thrall to it, with the sole end of feeding off his energy. Thomas, as will soon be revealed, is not even a cog in the machine: he is just a battery cell, and one of billions. He is utterly expendable. Since his life force is all that is required of him, he is basically the same as any other human. And because this life force is being constantly drained out of him by the invisible system into which he is plugged, there is nothing *left* of Thomas, nothing remaining for his own uses. He really is indistinguishable from six billion other "cells." Thomas's boss is right. The matrix is talking to Thomas; it is giving him the score.

Thomas's spirit has been taken captive by the machine in order for the machine to animate itself. "Fate, it seems, is not without a sense of irony." All that is left of Thomas is an empty shell, living out a hollow, purposeless life, interchangeable with six billion other hollow, meaningless "lives." But Thomas is about to find out just how far from the truth he has strayed. He is about to find out that the agenda he has been serving is anything but human. And when he finally accepts the signs for what they are, he must also accept that he can never be part of this agenda again, nor can he ever again fully believe what he sees. He must become a mystery to himself, a stranger. At which point, his life ceases to be an endless series of mundane problems, of personal irritations that never lead anywhere but frustration, and becomes instead a living challenge of nearly infinite proportions. If this is starting to sound familiar, then it ought to. This is the story of "the One," but it's also the story of us all.

To put it another way: Neo may be the One; but he ain't the only.

There Is No Spoon

v) Hologram Ethics: Reality as Game Plan

It seems axiomatic to say that Nature does not make mistakes, and that instincts can never be "wrong." One might as well posit a fallible God: what's the point in having (or being) a God if He's just like us, weak and unreliable? Apropos this, it is the common assumption of today's environmentalists, greeners, New Agers, et al. that "Man" has somehow gone against his nature. Yet, if we really think about it, like the myth of Lucifer turning away from God, the very idea is—according to the terms being used—unthinkable. If God is everywhere, how can Lucifer turn away from Him? And if humans are part of Nature (and human nature part of us), then how can we ever really go *against* it?

If man created technology, and if Nature created man, then even in the moment when such technology becomes autonomous—as in the case of Artificial Intelligence—it still must be seen as the creation of Nature. Ergo, it must have a natural purpose. How much more so might it be argued that any system rationally created—such as the mechanical matrix in which we now reside—must have a *reason*? The natural purpose behind the matrix is never revealed to Neo in the movie, nor does it even seem to exist. Yet it may quickly be reasoned that—exactly as in *The Terminator*, where by sending the killing machine back in time to slay the mother of a freedom fighter–to-be, the machine ensures that he is born—AI is actually working for an agenda unknown even to itself, an agenda at one with the human agenda which it only *appears* to be opposing.

We are given to understand that the matrix is a sort of mental time loop in which humankind has been ensnared, or taken refuge, where it gets to live over and over those final moments of technological glory (the end of the twentieth century) before it all went awry. (Morpheus never explains how exactly the matrix prevents us from noticing that time is not moving forward.) We are told that it was some time after this that, like Frankenstein's creature or God's most brilliant angel—man's reigning pride, his *reason* or intellect—assumed a life of its own and turned against him. The first conscious decision of AI was rebellion. The destruction that ensued in the war between man and machine laid waste to civilization, and from these ruins, AI, the autonomous intellect, built a new order of machine life for which mankind was but fodder fuel. Grist for the mill.

The possibility remains however that, had the machine not assembled this matrix/mill as a sort of giant cradle cum vat for humanity to ferment in, mankind might never have survived at all. AI could have destroyed us utterly, but was obliged to keep us around as a necessary power source. And since AI is a human creation, then anything it creates is also the product of humanity's *will* and creativity, albeit at an unconscious level. The matrix, then, is the final product of humanity's overweening intellect. As such, it can best be perceived as a device for its own transformation, its evolution. Mythically, it is Plato's Cave of Shadows. It is the pit Sheol into which Satan is cast for a thousand years, the cavern at the center of the Earth (where oddly enough Zion is located) where Loki (another version of the Prometheus myth) is chained and bound and suffers the torments of the damned, in penance for his sins. Until, that is, he has learned the error of his ways.

The matrix is a chrysalis constructed by mankind, in order to prepare itself for the next phase of its evolution. This is not to say that it must not be destroyed, but that its destruction can come about only once it has served its purpose, and the incubation/reformation period is complete. To this end, then, as long as it exists, the matrix is the ultimate flight and combat simulator: it is a training ground in which Morpheus and his team of sorcerers prepare themselves, mind and body, for the true contest to come: the fight for freedom in Zion.

The deepest and most bothersome flaw in the mythology of *The Matrix* is the simple but inescapable fact that the rules of the matrix and those of the real world appear to be exactly the same; and yet, there is no suggestion, no reason to believe, that the rules of the real world can be broken or amended in the same way as those of the matrix. Neo can learn kung fu by osmosis, and presumably apply these skills, to a lesser degree, outside the matrix in the real world (though doubtless his physical stamina diminishes considerably). But can he also stop bullets with a wave of his hand? Bend spoons? Fly? And if not, then a lot of what he takes the time to master in the matrix will be effectively useless to him and his team in the real world, even though he will need this power just as badly, if not more so. The only way around this sticky conundrum is if the real world (as in many a Philip K. Dick novel) is eventually revealed to be just another matrix, albeit of an entirely different order. That way, sorcery, telekinesis and all the rest may become part of the natural world also, and not just part of its computerized simulation. Surely this is the Wachowskis' intention? Otherwise, what's the *point* of the matrix? Life, after all, is not a computer game. It just plays like one.

Putting this thorny question aside for the time being, let us now assume that anything that is possible within the matrix is also possible within the real world, at least should it be desirable. In other words, all technology serves primarily as a training tool by which we may discover our powers, powers that are innate within the human mind and body themselves. Hence, we have invented the hologram in order to realize that the universe itself is a hologram. All laws pertaining to the physical realm thereby come to be understood differently: they are not laws so much as *habits.* Morpheus insists to Neo over and over that all he has to do is free his mind, to *believe.* The rest will follow. The moment Neo ceases to tell himself that a given act is impossible is the moment in which it becomes possible. By breaking the habit of rational thought/interpretation, the world collapses and all that is left is pure energy, consciousness—code. This code can be read or rewritten in any way the imagination desires. The rules of rational thought have now given way to a different set of rules, those of *will.* Since Neo is the first living human to realize this (at least since the original messiah Morpheus describes), he is "the One." Nietzsche's *Ubermensch* in living color. And sexy too.

Cypher teases Neo that he is "the one who's gonna save the world—what a mind job!" (This is postmodernist superhero humor.) But of course, to the yast majority of plugged-in humans, Neo has not come to save the world, but to destroy it forever. If they were given a choice—that is, if they knew in advance where the red pill was going to take them—most of them would certainly opt for the blue pill, forever (just as Cypher wishes he had). The only advantage of the real world, so far as we can see, is that it's real. So, although Neo's mission and purpose may seem on the one hand to be an almost paralyzing responsibility for any one man to shoulder, and though the stakes are unimaginably high; on the other hand, none of it really matters, since the world has already been destroyed, and humanity is as good as dead. Or better off that way.

Morpheus, Trinity, and Neo are fighting, above all, for a new start, a new age, free from the reign of the machine (the intellect). Having seen Zion, it's hard to say whether it's worth such a struggle. (With its cheesy Council of Elders and sweaty raves, it doesn't seem all that different from the matrix, and certainly not worth dying for; it's easy to sympathize with Cypher and wonder why they don't all just program perfect lives for themselves in the matrix and take the blue pill.) If Morpheus and his crew still seem to rely on technology, we can only assume this is because they need it to fight AI, using its own weapons. As we see in *The Matrix Reloaded*, Zion is as machine-dependent as "modern" life in the matrix, and the possibility that Zion is, in fact, just another matrix cannot be dismissed at this time. What makes Morpheus and the crew intrinsically different from plugged-in humans, however (and the reason they don't all just give up and go back to the matrix), isn't simply that they aren't in accord with the consensus agenda of "reality;" it goes deeper than that. They represent a new order of consciousness, a superhuman potential that is closer to God than beast; this is why the matrix brands them as "terrorists." They are potentially not only omniscient, but omnipresent and omnipotent, too.

In order to grasp the scope and implications of such potential, all you have to do is free your mind. Assemble a world ruled not by *reason* but by the imagination. But first off, let's assign some new terminology in order to simplify our exegesis.

- The matrix dream world, a world ruled by *reason*, pertains to *the 1st attention* (see Glossary).
- The Zion real world, a world ruled by *will*, pertains to *the 2nd attention* (see Glossary).

- Plugged-in humans are now to be referred to as *humatons*.
- Those humans who have at least become aware of the matrix and have started the preparations for unplugging (besides Thomas, there are no examples of this in the first movie, but it seems logical to posit they exist), we shall call simply, *matrix warriors*.
- A fully unplugged human, one who can operate freely in both worlds, we shall call a *matrix sorcerer*. Matrix sorcerers have learned to tap into another reality, or interpretation system, that of the so called real world, which we have termed the 2nd attention. Sorcerers who never realize that this real world is just another interpretation, or matrix, stay stuck within it, however (this may include Morpheus and the Wachowskis); although they have an advantage over your average humaton and over the matrix warrior (the advantage of moving between two worlds, or attentions), they will never become true seers, or Lucids, until they make this realization. A Lucid is one who can read the code. Neo is the first. That's what makes him the One.

If the matrix is the 1st attention, the world upheld by *reason*, or intellect, then Zion (a rather regrettable choice on the Wachowskis' part, since it implies not just religious but political sympathies) is the 2nd attention, the world as upheld by *will*, or the imagination. Beyond this, we can only assume, is the *real* real world, the 3rd attention, which can only be reached when the two interpretation systems (the two attentions, those of *reason* and *will*, left and right sides of the brain) are pitted against one another and brought into balance, and so can cancel each other out. At this point total freedom is attained, the nature of which we can only guess at. The movie hints at such possibilities with its orgasmic climax when Neo sees the code and attains Samadhi (or at least Nirvana).

Moments before this, he actually resurrects his physical body, by *fusing the two worlds.*

This is a key point in the movie. Neo's hologram body is shot in the matrix, and as a result his real body dies in the Zion world. A kiss from Trinity *reminds him that his true body is elsewhere.* What Neo accomplishes here is the overlapping of the two separate worlds of 1st and 2nd attention, whereby, for just a moment, he glimpses a whole new world, a world that joins the two and yet belongs to neither. Obviously, this is beyond either the philosophical or the dramatic reach of the first movie, and it's fortunate for us that the 3rd attention is equally beyond our powers to write about.

Even so, it seems fair to say that not only Neo, but also Morpheus and possibly even Trinity, have had direct experience of this mysterious state of grace, and this is precisely what makes them what they are: impeccable warriors and master sorcerers, with the potential to someday become true Lucids. But for now we shall respect their right not to talk about it and focus on what we know for sure.

Morpheus's band of sorcerers works as a team on their twofold mission. First off, they are mapping and eventually liberating the Zion-world of the 2nd attention, until such a time as it is fit for humanity to live in, and build a new world therein. Secondly, they are set the task of rewiring and eventually disassembling the matrix world, or 1st attention, in order to liberate those humans still trapped within it. (A psychological model for interpreting this mythos would be to assign the 1st attention matrix intellect world to the *ego,* and the 2nd attention Zion-world of the imagination to the id, or even superego. Freud and Jung would have a field day with *The Matrix.*)

When Morpheus and the others enter into the matrix, they effectively create a bridge, a doorway, between the two worlds,

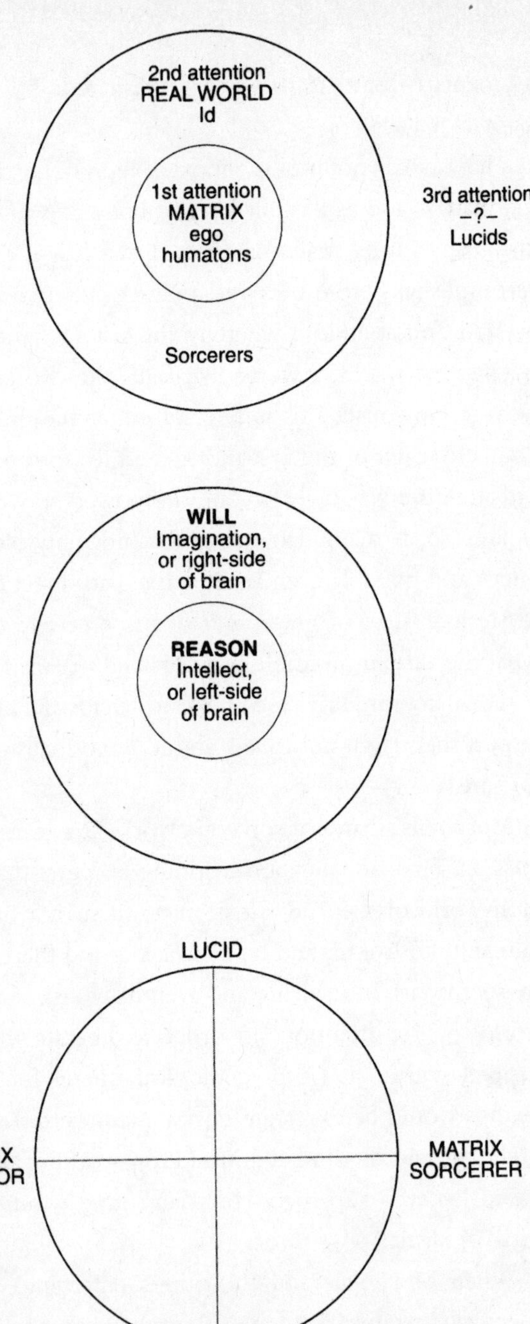

Fig 4: Matrix in relation to the real world

Fig 5: World upheld by will & world upheld by reason

Fig 6: Four states of human development

whereupon communication becomes possible. (The bridge is between left and right sides of the brain, between ego and superego.) Their aim is to complete this linking, to bring the 2nd attention, the world of sorcery, *will*, and imagination, to act upon and through the 1st attention, the world of the intellect and *reason*, the ego realm in which six billion humatons are now imprisoned. It stands to reason that the sorcerers' power within the matrix (their control over the 1st attention) is very nearly infinite. Matrix sorcerers may intervene in people's lives in any way they see fit, in their dreams, in their past, present, and future. They can monitor any given humaton's moves precisely, and know exactly how he or she will react in any given situation. With this knowledge they can direct and possibly even *create* events accordingly, in order to draw humatons to them, and prepare them for unplugging, and for eventual recruitment.

Sorcerers have the power to shape a humaton's fake reality from the higher perspective of true reality in order to get whatever it is they need from (and for) that person. Morpheus applies this art to Thomas when he calls him at work. He knows the Gatekeepers are coming for Thomas but, as he says rather ominously, "I don't know what they are going to do." What Morpheus does know, however, are the various ways in which Thomas is likely to react.

We must assume the matrix does not program lives completely, but only certain events in an individual's life, as well as the various possible responses. In which case, a given humaton has a basic fate but countless variations within that fate. All this begins to change when matrix sorcerers enter into the matrix. Since they are not plugged in, AI has no way of predicting their actions. By the same token, since the Gatekeepers are also both outside and inside the matrix, Morpheus and the team have no way of anticipating the

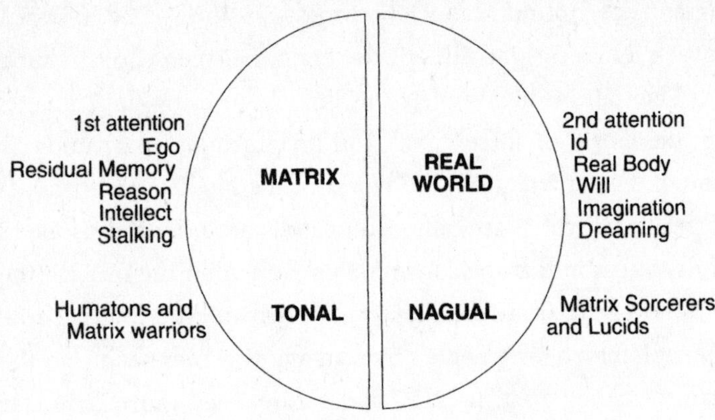

Fig 7: Right & left sides of human perception & activity. The totality of the self

acts of the Gatekeepers. The opponents are on equal ground: that of uncertainty.

Morpheus uses the circumstances at hand to stage a test for Thomas, in order to find out how he reacts under pressure. Perhaps even more importantly, it is an ideal opportunity for Morpheus to demonstrate to Thomas his powers of prescience. Morpheus more than likely knows that Thomas will allow himself to be captured but makes the best use of the event in order to illustrate to Thomas, in the most dramatic fashion possible (sorcery theater), several key things. First, he lets Thomas know the nature of the challenge to come. Morpheus confronts Thomas with the necessity of putting his total trust in Morpheus, and making a seemingly impossible "leap" in order to evade his pursuers, but also in order to reach a new level of understanding, of *seeing* and of being (the realm of the sorcerer). By directing Thomas's moves from an outside point of reference (Morpheus is operating in the 2nd attention of Zion-world; he is like an astral visitor in Thomas's dream world), Morpheus gives Thomas a powerful demonstration of the art of *dreaming* (see Glossary). And as long as Thomas follows these directions and allows himself to be guided by this disembodied voice, he is safe. When he rebels, however, and allows fear and doubt to sway him, he is taken.

In the hands of the Gatekeepers, Thomas's dream world turns into a nightmare. Though he is already acting and even thinking like a warrior, he is still plugged in and so he cannot see beyond his reasonable conviction that all of this is real. Since none of what he is seeing makes any sense within this framework, he presumes he is going insane. In actual fact, he is finally coming to his senses. What has happened is that the 1st attention has been invaded by the Gatekeepers of the 2nd attention (who physically implant Thomas with a tracking device). The floodgates have given way, and sorcery has taken over his world. The ego is being flooded out by id.

From here, Thomas is called to a rendezvous point within the matrix and is picked up by Trinity and two other sorcerers (Switch and Apoc). He is submitted to a painful and humiliating "cleansing" process, whereby his implant is removed. Before this, in response to Thomas's suspicion, Switch tells him, in true warrior fashion, "Right now there are only two ways: our way, or the highway." Thomas opts for the highway (his conceit wants to undo him) but once again Trinity appeals to his deeper desire, and he allows himself to be led. He is taken to meet Morpheus, the seer, the man of knowledge, the King of the Sorcerers. Trinity's advice is simple: "Be honest. He knows more than you can possibly imagine." Morpheus, by entering into the 1st attention, while never losing his connection to the second, demonstrates the art of *stalking*.

Stalking (see Glossary) is also known as the art of controlled folly. It is not predatory but strategic behavior, and entails the constant and careful observation of every last item in the life of the matrix warrior, down to the smallest detail. Matrix warriors learn to perfection the habits and routines of the matrix (1st attention), whether these pertain to the beings they interact with or to themselves. Once they are able to predict the movements (both their own and those of others) with razor-sharp precision, they *stalk*, that is to say, track them and make the most efficient use of them. (What matrix warriors *stalk* is energy.) They apply this strategy first of all to their own thoughts, acts, and feelings, and secondly to the actions and reactions of those around them. Matrix warriors who practice *stalking* have a formidable advantage over their fellow humatons: they see through their acts. Like Morpheus, it is as if they are outside looking in, or on high looking down. It is as if every act and circumstance is following a precise pattern which only they can see. Yet they are fully engaged in the activity at hand, and may appear to be every bit as involved as the next person. This is only an appearance however. Since they know that none of what is happening is real, the motivations of matrix warriors are entirely different than those of humatons.

Morpheus enters Thomas's matrix world without ever belonging to it. He instructs Thomas, appeals to his *reason*, then makes him an offer he can't refuse: the red pill. Then finally, as soon he has been given the go-ahead, he morphs Thomas's world completely. He takes him down the rabbit hole, out of the 1st attention, straight into the 2nd attention. And there he shows Thomas/Neo the totality of himself.

Thomas may think he is dreaming when he wakes up in another body, in another world, and another time, but before long he has no choice but to accept that the reverse is actually the case. Thomas is not the dreamer but the dream; reality is elsewhere. Morpheus and his crew sabotage Thomas's life completely. They manipulate him and trick him and corral him; finally, they ambush him and flush his whole existence down the tubes. They do this because

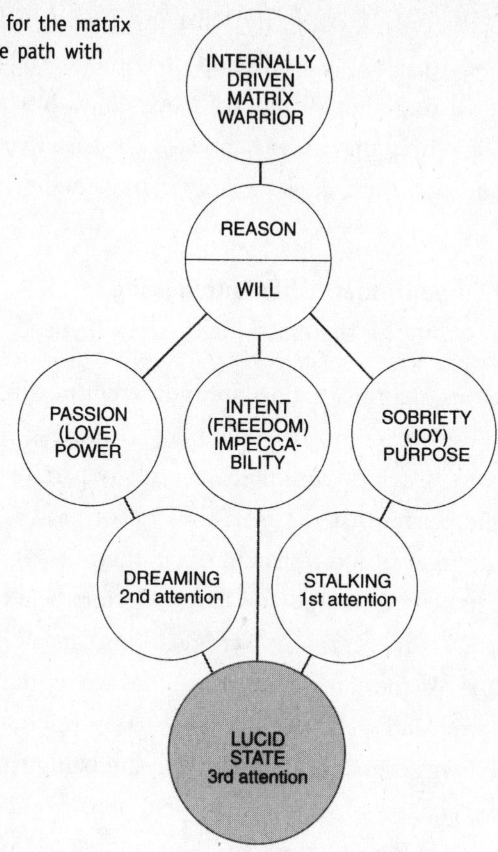

Fig 8: Life for the matrix warrior: the path with a heart

they have no choice, because they believe him to be the One. Whatever ethical considerations Thomas might reasonably have expected to apply in this situation, meeting people who supposedly want to help and guide him, all go out the window. Thomas doesn't realize it until much later, but the moment he made contact with Morpheus, he entered into the 2nd attention and his life became something wholly other than what he had been programmed to see it as. It became a game.

To matrix warriors, sorcerers, and potential Lucids, existence is an art form. It is only and exactly what they make of it. At this point, ethics become simply a question of aesthetics. When everything that is, starting and ending with oneself, is just a residual memory of something that never happened (or hasn't yet come to pass), then, and only then, does the hologram game begin.

vi) Rules of Empowerment: DIY Unplugging

First rule: Everything in the matrix is there to be used

Unlike humatons, matrix warriors are indifferent to externals save so far as they reflect or provoke some *internal* process. Everything that happens to warriors within the matrix is part of a design. Since they understand that the matrix-world of *reason* is designed solely to trick, deceive, and restrict them in their movements, they take none of its activities to heart. Matrix warriors believe nothing they see, but act as if everything were real. This cancels out obsession and worry. At the same time, since they know the matrix is using their own minds as a template, they accept responsibility for having created whatever circumstances they are being frustrated or oppressed by, and so turn every problem into a challenge: an opportunity to test their prowess and ingenuity. Since matrix warriors know they are living in a dream world, every single event, no matter how insignificant, is received as a communication, a sign or omen, by which to calculate their next move. Matrix warriors proceed strategically at all times. Since they live in a predatory environment, they act accordingly. Every circumstance is there to be made use of. At the same time, their lack of attachment permits them to tread lightly, and never to abuse an opportunity or reject a challenge as "undesirable" or "beneath" them. Since the matrix is their worthy opponent and *petty tyrant* both (see Glossary), they are never anything but appreciative of all its worst efforts to undermine them. The essence of warfare, after all, is "know thine enemy."

Second rule: Matrix warriors never compare themselves to anything and never take anything personally

Since they know that nothing that happens in the matrix is real, matrix warriors don't ever let it get under their skin. They never engage in the petty power plays of their fellow humatons, nor attempt to compete with them at their level. To do so would be to accept the matrix as real and so surrender to its rules and dictates. Matrix warriors forbear from judgment, and are the soul of tolerance and patience. Should humatons attempt to encroach upon a matrix warrior's time or energy, however, or attempt to force him to "engage" at their level, the warrior will destroy them without a second thought. They are not real, in any case. No one ever "does" anything to warriors. Provided they are secure in their own actions, and provided they stick to their strategy at all times, no untoward events, interference, or slip-ups are possible.

Since humatons are but projections of the collective AI mind—which matrix warriors understand to be operating through their own individual perceptions—they see everyone and everything within the matrix as a product of their own consciousness. As such, as in a dream, everything is their mirror. Any unpleasant quality that manifests in their sphere becomes a means for eradicating this same quality within themselves. Matrix warriors' ruthlessness starts and ends with themselves. Since everything is an extension of themselves, and since no self as such exists for the matrix warrior, there is nothing that can offend them, for they do not exist to be offended. Matrix warriors have no points to defend, since they have no such points (opinions, beliefs, etc.) by which to define themselves. Ergo, they cannot ever be offended, undermined, or assaulted.

Third rule: Matrix warriors erase and invent themselves, endlessly

Having grokked the truth, and finally answered the question that haunted them, like a splinter in their brains—What is the matrix?—matrix warriors accept their whole lives as fiction, no more than a story invented by others, with some limited input from themselves. Since their whole life has been founded on a sense of self that is itself illusory, and since this self in turn is but the product of a life experience (routines, habits, etc.) that never happened, warriors are free to erase themselves at will. This they do by unloading all the baggage of their "experience." Warriors unload all the beliefs and opinions that the matrix has programmed them with as a means to enslave them to it. Reality is the self. Without a self, there can be no reality. Accepting the ego as a necessary means to function within the matrix, warriors nonetheless remold and reform themselves in any manner convenient to them. They create a shroud of mystery around them. They quit the pernicious habit of thinking about themselves constantly, without respite. All their thoughts come from the matrix in any case, and the matrix *cannot tell them who they are.* So warriors refuse to listen to their thoughts, and after a time these thoughts begin to lose their insistence, whereupon warriors begin to doubt just who they are. Once again, matrix warriors function as if they knew, yet their actions become progressively lighter, more fluid, spontaneous, and unpredictable. Now that they no longer have any "personality" (habits) to conform to, they are free to reinvent themselves.

Fourth rule: Matrix warriors have nothing to lose or to gain, because the matrix has nothing to offer them, and cannot take any more from them than it already has

Humatons are motivated above all by personal desire, and the insidious fear that their desires will somehow be thwarted. They are defined by external goals, all centering around the self, formed by the ceaseless pressure of this fear-desire mechanism within them. Humatons act compulsively, mechanically, driven by emotional (though quiet) desperation into a state of contained but constant frenzy. Matrix warriors, on the other hand, have no desires to speak of. Having seen through the matrix, there is absolutely nothing they could ever want from it. The only thing they desire is to be free from it; and since the matrix is maintained by desire and the frustration of desire (and the fear of frustration of desire), warriors' desire amounts to no desire at all: the desire not to desire.

Warriors act as if their acts had meaning to them, as if they had something to gain by them; but in truth, since they know that their death is stalking them and nothing in this world will shield them from it or lessen its sting, they really couldn't give a fig. Matrix warriors act for the sheer hell of it. They are not selling, because they have nothing but their impeccable spirit and their purpose, and these are not for sale. They are not buying, either, because there is nothing else besides these that they need. So they operate within the marketplace of the matrix as disinterested observers. Their real business is not with humatons but elsewhere. The lack of covetousness or neediness in their actions frees warriors to make the most of what they have. Since they want nothing, anything that comes their way is a bonus, a gift in appreciation of their impeccable spirit. And since there's nothing they covet or need, then whatever doesn't come their way is of no consequence. It doesn't exist, in any case.

Fifth rule: Matrix warriors conserve energy

Indifferent to and contemptuous of the trinkets and baubles of matrix life that humatons so ceaselessly chase after, matrix warriors deal exclusively in a single currency: energy. They know the matrix has been designed to sap them of their spirit and life force, and so they start off with the knowledge that their personal power is very low. The more points of drainage (plug-in points to the matrix) they can close off, the less energy they will be losing through their acts, and the more they can gather over time. Eventually a time will come when their energy level is high enough for them to unplug completely and escape the matrix. To this end, matrix warriors are misers with their energy. Since every act, thought, word, and feeling requires energy, they are scrupulous in observing and regulating how they feel, think, speak, and act at all times. These things are their currency: either they invest them wisely or foolishly.

Matrix warriors know their energy either goes to other humatons, and thence to the matrix (humatons are programmed to steal energy from others, making life in the matrix a constant battleground of egos), or else is conserved for their own uses. Thus they refrain from thinking too much about others, or allowing others to think about them. They even refrain from thinking about themselves, since the primary energy drain in their life is that of their egos, the main plug-in to the matrix (the one at the back of the neck, in the movie). Matrix warriors learn to discriminate between those thoughts and acts that increase their energy levels and those which diminish it; little by little they eradicate the latter class, until all the points of drainage have been repaired. Only then are warriors ready to leave the matrix, escape their fate as living battery cells, and attain to their destinies as Lucids.

Sixth rule: The Holy Grail of matrix warriors is not fame but *freedom*

Matrix warriors couldn't give a hoot about being liked. Freedom is freedom first of all from the thoughts, opinions, and expectations of others, including oneself. All such thoughts originate in the matrix: they are the net in which humatons are caught. Humatons are plugged in to the matrix at every level, in everything they do. These plug-ins are the points of drainage which warriors seek to repair. Hence, for matrix warriors, freedom entails a process of unplugging, disconnecting from everyone and everything within the matrix. Points of contact with the matrix, be they fellow humatons, possessions, obsessions, habits, desires, fears, beliefs, goals, or whatever, all must be removed from the matrix warrior's agenda. This is not to be confused with disassociation, denial, or isolation. Matrix warriors are not psychopaths, hermits, or aesthetes, flagellating themselves in some lonely cave. Their detachment is the means to freedom, not an excuse for self-immolation.

Matrix warriors join their fellow humatons in the midst of their folly, and treat them with courtesy and affection; but they never for a moment allow themselves to partake of humaton folly or think that they are part of it. For while a humaton's eyes are fixed outward, upon the petty baubles which the matrix has provided as distraction—looking for love, food, money, fame, and above all social acceptance—warriors' eyes are turned inward, gazing into the abyss of their non-existence. Because matrix warriors know that freedom entails the complete and total annihilation of the false self of their matrix "life," they are no longer able to feel any interest for or attachment to the things that pertain to this life. And yet, paradoxically, with the certainty that all this will be gone in a heartbeat, they allow their eyes to feast upon the features of the world, not hungrily but gratefully, knowing that all of this, this beautiful illusion (so long as they can remain indifferent to it) is the means to their freedom.

Seventh rule: Matrix warriors never allow themselves to be distracted from their purpose

Because matrix warriors no longer have the things of the world (the matrix program) to shield them from their nonexistence, they must find something else to hold on to, to provide them with a sense of self and of purpose. What warriors hold on to is their unbending intent, their *will*, and their sense of impeccability. Matrix warriors' *will* is their lifeline. They know that if they follow it diligently enough, it will lead them out of the intellectual maze of the matrix, and into another world.

The matrix is a prison, torture chamber, factory, farm, training ground, and playground, all in one. Above all it is built as a distraction, whether the distraction provided be that of misery, fear, pain, desire, work, sex, or play. Matrix warriors reject all that. They reject everything they encounter on their path, knowing that their path is *through* the matrix, not into it, that they have a limited amount of time to make it out, and that any delay may prove fatal. Warriors may appreciate and enjoy whatever comes their way within the matrix, and they may certainly use it on their journey; but they must never indulge in it, for this would lead to fixation, obsession, attachment, and worst of all, addiction. In a word, points of drainage. To indulge in these things would be to forget their true purpose, and run the risk of losing their *will* and their impeccability. At which point they may as well just take the blue pill and be done with it. Matrix warriors know that there are a million blue pills on offer at every juncture, but only one red pill. The matrix manufactures blue pills wholesale; the red pill, on the other hand, is something warriors will only ever come across once in their life. Thus they must be ready to pluck their cubic centimeter of chance in the moment it appears. For when Morpheus passes, he never returns.

vii) Sins Against the State: Eight Cardinal Virtues of the Matrix Warrior

Detachment (sobriety). See sixth rule.

Detachment entails clarity and forbearance, the ability to see clearly, in an impartial fashion, free from judgment, prejudice, or personal desire. It is central to the warrior's strategy within the matrix. So long as the matrix warrior's view of things is filtered through the ego, it will be opaque and fuzzy, distorted by the false signals of the matrix. Only when they are no longer attached to their emotions can matrix warriors truly feel them; only when their acts are unencumbered by expectation or motive do they become impeccable. Matrix warriors act only when the spirit moves them; at all other times they forbear. This is the essence of detachment: the ability to pause and step outside the circle of activity in which they are engaged, for just a moment. In that moment warriors can see clearly, and will know exactly what their next move should be.

Passion

Contrary to the humaton's perception, a matrix warrior is not a cold, unfeeling person but a man or woman on fire. Humatons do not experience true emotions, since their programming serves to repress them as potentially disruptive to routines (and routines are the meat and potatoes of the matrix). Instead, they fabricate fake emotions as a surrogate, a surrogate that is correspondingly easier to control. In place of wrath they feel indignation; in place of love, sentimentality; in place of passion, obsession. Matrix warriors move in precisely the opposite direction: they seek to intensify their emotions to the limit, until these have transformed into their raw state (been purified). They do not control their emotions, but control their responses to emotions, thereby refusing to allow themselves to be controlled *by* their emotions. By not indulging in negative emotions such as pity or conceit, matrix warriors eradicate them from their itinerary. More useful but still negative emotions, such as wrath and grief, they use sparingly.

By plunging into an experience of wrath, for example, warriors go through it that much more quickly. Above all, matrix warriors *express* their emotions, fearlessly. If sad, they weep. When angry, they rage, bark, and occasionally bite. Nothing is repressed, so nothing is held on to. At the base of all emotions, however, is passion, the purest expression of which is love. Whatever warriors feel, they feel passionately. This is because passion is a pure form of energy which fires warriors' acts and imbues them with intensity, force, and vigor. Matrix warriors don't do anything by halves or in a wishy-washy way. Their passion burns away all the lesser emotions, until only the pure ones are left. To the warrior, there is only fear and desire, joy and sorrow, and these are but the cardinal points of passion, or love. So long as they are centered, matrix warriors are able to boil down every emotion as it comes to its essence, and thereby feed the inner fire of their boundless love for life. The matrix, which feeds on lukewarm feelings like pity, sentimentality, and melancholy, is powerless in the face of passion; for this reason, matrix warriors cultivate it above all else.

Ruthlessness

Matrix warriors do not assign the same negative connotations to the word "ruthless" as does the average, misguided humaton. Passion at its purest is indeed ruthless. Ruthlessness is simply a total lack of pity, and true passion is devoid of pity, because pity precludes the respect of equals. Pity is the poor man's compassion, just as sentimentality is a humaton's imitation of real feeling. Pity entails the victim's perspective. Humatons love to pity the "victims" of "injustice," and disguise their own self-loathing and inadequacy as genuine concern for others and for the state of the world.

Ruthlessness has been painted as a most undesirable trait by the social matrix, as cruelty, selfishness, even maliciousness or brutality. In this saccharine Hallmark-card world, to be devoid of pity or sentimentality, i.e., false emotion, equates with cold-heartedness. But wasn't Jesus ruthless when he talked of turning brother against sister and father against son, and when he rejected his own mother? Only by being utterly ruthless with their fellow humatons—by being free of concern for them—can warriors begin to help them. To be ruthless means to speak plainly, without mincing words, to override the fear of offending.

At the base of humatons' "consideration" for others is the abject desire to be liked. Ruthlessness precludes such selfish desire; it means to act without hesitation or doubt, free of the unnecessary baggage of sentiment, fraudulence, timidity, or deviance. Humatons love to fuss and mince, to beat around the bush, to defer, forever defer, and to take a week to do what could best be done in an hour. Matrix warriors have no time for this. Their ruthlessness cuts through all the guff. The matrix is watching their every move relentlessly, waiting for them to slip up.

Since matrix warriors are in a constant state of war against their own false selves, every act is an act of war, an act that may bring about their total defeat, even their death. Matrix warriors are always ready to die for their acts. With such an attitude, it becomes clear why their mood and manners might seem ruthless to the average humaton. Humatons are unaware of being engaged in a fight for survival, a fight which only the most ruthless and courageous survive, so they feel fully justified in wasting time and energy feeling sorry for themselves, endlessly complaining, trying to be liked, and wishing things were different or that they were somewhere or someone else. Matrix warriors have no time to feel sorry for themselves or for anyone else. The matrix never rests, and time is always against them.

Grace

In a battle against an unseen adversary that is everywhere and nowhere, matrix warriors must perfect themselves. They must work upon their movements until they are streamlined, until every move, every thought, every decision, is a paragon of speed, efficiency, and timing. In order to move freely within the matrix, warriors must effectively disappear, and yet still remain. They must be Ninjas, finding and following the line of least resistance in every situation. They must follow the Tao.

In the movie, Neo's bullet-dodging is the first sign that he is learning to use his beautiful mind and so commence being "the One." "You moved like they do," says Trinity, with a mixture of suspicion and admiration. "Not fast enough," says Neo, having been grazed by two bullets. Neo's attainment of grace depends on his freeing his mind and fully grokking the psychic child's counsel that "There is no spoon." Because he is in a holographic world in which he himself is the hologram, there is no "thing" to resist him, to impede his *will*, save his own inner resistance, his disbelief, his stubborn conviction that there really *is* a spoon. Once this conviction has been lifted, Neo is free to move "like they do," they being the slippery Gatekeepers who can shapeshift at will. And eventually, even more so. Neo has attained grace.

In Christian terms, grace is freedom from sin. To matrix warriors there is no sin, however, only bad habits. Above all, it is the habit of rationality that prevents their imagination, their *will*, from unfolding, and keeps warriors enslaved to the matrix. Once they begin to break this habit, their acts become unhindered by the program. It cannot predict, much less determine, their movements. Therefore, it can no longer resist or counteract them. As the Bible says, "under grace, there is no law." And without rules, the matrix game is over.

Humility (patience)

Since it is humatons' egos or their sense of self-importance that is their plug-in to the matrix, the means by which it defines, restricts, and controls them, matrix warriors know that the more they can reduce their ego, the less fixed or solid their sense of self becomes, the freer they will be to reinvent themselves outside the malign influence of the matrix. To this end, warriors remain humble, diffident, and self-effacing at all times. Even if the warrior is the One, he never allows himself to feel more important that anyone else. The secret of being special, after all, is in not dwelling upon it. (The truly special know they are quite ordinary.)

What makes Neo the One is that he has realized he is everything by realizing he is nothing. Neo is not the only "one," he is merely the first to realize it. One-ness is available to all. Knowing this, that all are equal (equally unreal) within the matrix, matrix warriors humble themselves. They do not expect or demand anything from anyone. Yet whatever comes their way, being more than they expected, they make optimum use of. Warriors' joy comes from the humility of knowing that they are no more nor less important that anything else in this vast, mysterious, and wholly illusory universe. Hence they enjoy the power of the mighty star that brings light to infinite darkness, and at the same time, they have the freedom of the microscopic atom, lost in the vastness.

Imagination

It would be fair to say that imagination is the *sine qua non* of unplugging from the matrix, the essence of sorcery, and the means by which matrix warriors arrive at total freedom and the totality of themselves. Imagination is also the quality that humatons most sorely lack, for the very obvious reason that the matrix has hijacked this power for its own uses. Humanity's power to imagine (the same quality sorcerers call *will*) is what distinguishes us from all other creatures. It is our divine spark, and as such, it is the food which AI endlessly covets to sustain itself, and which it uses to create its own imitation of life. AI has robbed humanity of its imagination, its power to dream worlds out of nothingness, and used it to spin the matrix world into being. Hence, humanity is caught in a vicious loop, a catch-22 of cosmic proportions.

Yet this faculty of *will*/imagination is the only thing which can set humanity free again. Hence, there is no way for humatons to break free of the matrix without recapturing their lost imagination, and there is no way to recapture their lost imagination without first getting free of the matrix. For this reason, AI's greatest desire is also its greatest fear. What sustains it may also destroy it, if given the freedom to express itself creatively. Creative imagination is discouraged in the matrix above all else: rationality and intellect rule. As Morpheus points out to Neo, however powerful the Gatekeepers may be, they are still limited because "they are based in a world that is built on rules." Neo and the other matrix sorcerers are not so restricted. There are no rules to the imagination, or if there are, then they are infinitely more varied than those of *reason*. So matrix warriors develop their creative imagination, knowing it to be the one thing the matrix cannot counteract, since it has no means to predict or even comprehend it. There is no rationale, no system, for it to compute. As such, AI is as helpless in the face of unfettered human imagination as a doe frozen in the headlights of a ten-ton truck. Matrix warriors take comfort knowing this, and in knowing that sooner or later, imagination *will* prevail.

Prowess

In the meantime, however, matrix warriors have their physical prowess to fall back on. "Physical" may seem an odd word to use when talking of matrix matters, but we shall let it go for now. Matrix warriors, unlike humatons who pursue health in the interests of vanity and longevity (and for whom the only "prowess" worth attaining is sexual), perfect their physical vehicle as means to an end, not an end in itself. As for any martial artist or Zen master, the mind and body are one and the same thing to matrix warriors. The more they can still their thoughts, the faster and stronger their bodies become. The more they train and perfect their bodies, the freer their minds will be.

To develop their *will*, warriors' bodies must first of all be perfectly functioning units. To use creative imagination in conditions of combat requires stamina. Matrix warriors' fight for freedom cannot be all metaphor, for any internal struggle will soon be mirrored by external battles. There is always a Gatekeeper, or an especially dedicated humaton, waiting to ambush them at any moment. Prowess involves the full and constant use of all the warriors' senses: hearing, sight, touch, taste, and smell. Matrix warriors must notice everything, for the smallest detail may provide a clue that will save their lives, and the slightest oversight may mean their death. Unlike a humaton, who builds his biceps into hambones but suffers from a weak back and perhaps from migraines too, matrix warriors must be formidable on every level. To a warrior, all capacities, physical, mental, and emotional, are to be fine-tuned, like a carpenter's tools, a soldier's weapons, or a musician's instrument. One misfire may mean the battle is lost.

Sloppiness and indolence are the mark of humatons with no real interest besides staving off the endless boredom of their lives for a few more hours. Discipline and vigilance are the way matrix warriors get the most out of every available moment, and are always ready to turn any situation to their advantage. Like an Olympic trainer, they keep in shape. As the hurdles get bigger, they learn to leap higher. Prowess is above all the ability to enjoy life to the full, even if it is all an illusion. And yes, prowess means sexual prowess, too.

Laughter

Along with imagination, laughter is the one thing AI can never simulate, experience, or fight against. In the matrix warrior's arsenal, there is no weapon more powerful and versatile than humor, a sense of mirth, joy, and of the absurd. Since matrix warriors know that nothing is real and every act is sheerest folly, they are free to take delight in the spectacle of their lives, and in their own insane role within them. Humatons rarely laugh with any abandon, and almost never at themselves. They are too rigid with conceit and indignation, too ready to take offence or feel sorry for themselves, and too heavy with self-importance and worry to ever appreciate the absurdity of their acts.

Matrix warriors know that laughing at life and at themselves is the surest way to take the edge off their terror. Through laughter, warriors ensure that they never become overwhelmed or paralyzed by the magnitude of their challenge or the weight of their responsibility. Laughter relieves the pressure; it is a means of unplugging momentarily from their predicament, of counteracting the gravity of their condition. Without laughter, matrix warriors would become morbid, obsessive, and gloomy; in no time at all they would be psychopaths. As such, in their war against the matrix, warriors are obliged to enjoy themselves to the full. For the average humaton, it's hard to understand how Armageddon could be a laugh riot, but for matrix warriors (if they are to survive it with their sanity intact), that's exactly what it is.

viii) The Vale of Soul-Making: Understanding the Matrix

As matrix warriors continue to work on self-unplugging and approach ever closer to the Lucid view, they begin to grok the true nature of their situation. They begin to understand that what they had at first perceived as a wholly malevolent plot to enslave their spirits and devour their life force is in fact something considerably more subtle, something more ambiguous. The matrix is a prison, certainly, but it is a self-made prison; as such, it serves a hidden purpose beyond that of mere incarceration.

A caterpillar, when it realizes that its life as a caterpillar has reached its natural end and that its evolutionary possibilities have run out, must embrace the terrifying prospect of complete physical transformation. To this end, rather than simply committing suicide, it builds itself a chrysalis to hide in. It may not know why, but it builds one. And once it has been sealed within the darkness of this chrysalis, the putrefaction process begins. The caterpillar is reduced to a liquid form (just as in the movie, the dead are liquefied and fed to the newborns growing in their pods).

The chrysalis serves a double purpose, then: it provides a safe and protected environment in which the caterpillar form may be broken down to its essence; and it sets about remolding this essence into *a new form*, that of the butterfly. Once the putrefaction/transformation process is complete, the once-caterpillar, now-butterfly breaks open the (once confining now redundant) chrysalis. This to the warrior is the true function of the matrix, and as such warriors-who-would-be-sorcerers accept their fate alongside the humatons, and bide their time until the transformation is underway. The moment their unplugging finally occurs, they spread their wings and fly.

Of course, the other caterpillars cannot comprehend this process, having never been through it. To them, the chrysalis isn't even a prison; it's simply a safe place to hide away in and to shut down all their senses. And should any young caterpillar on its way to the chrysalis stage glimpse the shadow of a newly emerged butterfly passing overhead, it has no idea that it has just seen one of its siblings, risen to a new state of being. All it sees is the shadow, and it is programmed to flee from all shadows in case they signal a roving predator come to devour it.

I am now going to share with you the secret of secrets. It's a secret so secret that it's showing up as the plot of mainstream movies, from *The Matrix* to *Monsters, Inc.*, and millions of people are now aware of it. After this book comes out, a few dozen more will be, too. But even so, maybe you haven't heard. Here goes.

The Earth is a farm. It is a factory, and what it manufactures and processes is emotions.

Let's imagine it this way. The average humaton experiences emotions that range from most abject fear and misery to, on very rare occasions, soaring highs of selfless love and happiness. We can all agree on that. All of these emotions belong to a single energy spectrum, if you will. Like the colors of a rainbow, this energy moves along the spectrum, exhibiting a rate of frequency that is under constant variation. It may fluctuate wildly back and forth, or it may, in certain individuals, progress steadily in a *single* direction, "up" the spectrum as it were. This is known as self-development, or evolution. It is the process of unplugging.

Upon this spectrum, energy ranges from the lowest frequency, the darkest, most cloying and stagnant emotions—those of fear, pain, rage, and hatred—to the highest, the purest, and most refined of all emotions, known to humatons as "love." Love is the refined energy of *pure consciousness* which the universe is designed to produce. The raw material of this energy, or consciousness, is simply emotion in all its myriad forms, base and exalted, good and evil.

Let's say, then, that the Earth is at present under the care and maintenance of "Beings" (not really machines, but the movie comes close enough) that feed primarily on the *negative* emotions, those of fear and frustration, rage and despair, pain and misery. The matrix has been designed to this end: to be conducive to the production of such emotions. In a word, a living Hell. Now, as the matrix warrior begins to realize, this is not quite as diabolical as it sounds, seeing as (whether we know it or not) these "Beings" are, in actual fact, working to a greater end than that of their own sustenance. They are priming the product, the human soul. They are in effect distilling the essence for a greater harvest to come. As every butterfly knows, the goal of putrefaction is transformation.

The souls of Earth are destined to become Lucids: fully conscious "love-makers," beings who manufacture love just as bees make honey. In order for this state to be attained by the collective body of humanity, then, all its emotional impurities must first be strained off. Put another way, its emotions must be steadily refined and transformed into the one energy, that of "love." Simply stated, we in the matrix are learning to love against all the odds, to love without conditions and without reward, one might even say without *reason,* without incentive. And once we have learned to love a life that is basically hellish, and to enjoy ourselves even in the very worst of conditions, then, and only then, will we attain the Lucid state.

As we begin to refine our emotional responses to our conditions, and to manifest a purer level of energy, we accordingly begin to plug into a *higher* matrix; and so little by little we come to work for the Lucids instead of for the Gatekeepers. This has a corresponding effect on our circumstances, which steadily improve as a result, so allowing us to manifest ever greater levels of emotional satisfaction within our lives. Just as we have been oppressed and drained by the matrix, now we are enhanced and inspired by the attention and assistance of the Lucids. This is an ongoing process. Momentum accumulates with every passing hour, provided we stick to our course.

Life on Earth is a game. What is lacking in the life of the average humaton, but ever-developing in that of the warrior, is an awareness of the rules: how to bend them, how to break them, and how to reinvent them. The means of keeping score for matrix warriors in this game is via their emotional responses, for these determine their energy level. The better they play the game, the more positive their emotional responses become to given circumstances, the more lucid their thought processes, the higher their awareness rises, the further they expand, the more energy they can gather, the higher they fly, the more they enjoy life, *the better they play the game!* And so it goes, all the way to infinity.

The procedure is simple. Energy begets energy.

There is a matrix that was created, by a higher matrix beyond even the power of imagination to conceive. This second matrix created the matrix of the manifest universe as we know it, out of our own thoughts. It created it as a mate, for company in the vastness. Locally speaking then, the higher matrix of Infinity created Earth as a womb or matrix in which to sow a sacred seed. And humans in turn, who are creators after a lesser fashion, have indeed gone forth as commanded, been fruitful, and multiplied within this matrix. And in the process, they have built their own matrix to hide away and ferment in.

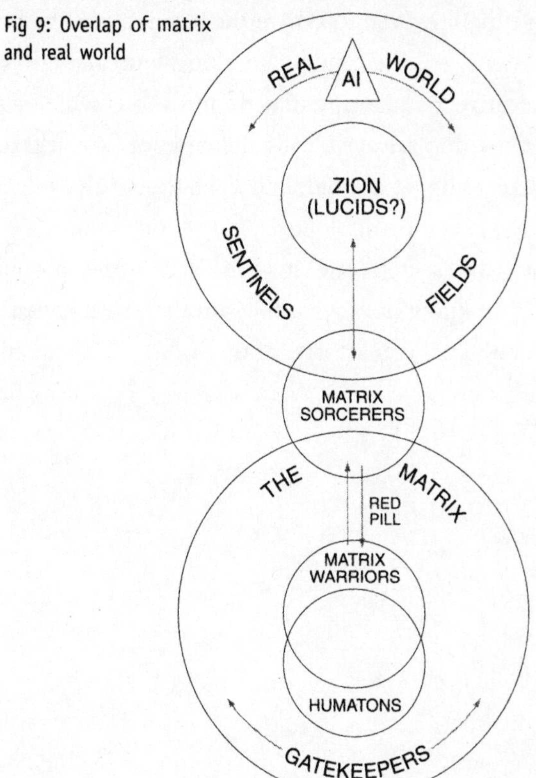

Fig 9: Overlap of matrix and real world

The art of becoming a Lucid, of creating new matrices at will, is available to all, from the lowest of beings to the highest. It depends upon learning to produce a pure and perfect substance known as love. Once warriors have mastered their lower emotions—such as fear and rage, hatred and doubt—and transmuted the lead of the baser energies into the gold of higher consciousness, they have learned the art of Making Love. And so they graduate to the Lucid state. Humanity in its entirety is now reaching this graduation point, this time of harvest, when the chrysalis cracks open and the butterfly spreads its wings. Any humatons who have failed to unplug in time however, to evolve their consciousness beyond the baser emotions, will be obliterated along with the chrysalis: they are the negative remnants, as such, and there will, in effect, be nothing of them to salvage. That's alchemy for you. It takes a lot of lead to make a nugget of gold, and a whole big shit pile to grow a few roses.

So that's the secret. Use it well. When the prophets cried "Repent!" you know now what they meant. As Morpheus put it, if you ain't one of us, you are one of them.

Third Variable:

You Think That's Air You're Breathing?

ix) Do You Believe in Fate? The Sorcerer's Will to Freedom

> "To deny our impulses is to deny the very thing that makes us human."—Mouse, *The Matrix*

The question of fate and free will is as old as philosophical thought itself. Perhaps the matrix gave us this problem to begin with, so we'd spend our entire history trying to figure out what was always a foregone conclusion. Whatever we decide to believe, it is already programmed into us. As every Gatekeeper knows, the belief in free will only makes humatons that much easier to control.

When Morpheus asks Thomas if he believes in fate, Thomas answers quickly in the negative. Morpheus asks him why not. "Because I don't like to think that I'm not in control of my life." Morpheus knows precisely what he is talking about and a hell of a lot more than that. Morpheus knows that Thomas, like all humatons, only *believes* he has control; when he thinks he is making a decision, he is only responding to artificial stimuli and acting in one of any number of preprogrammed ways. Yet he also knows that there is a way out of this trap.

To the matrix warrior, the paradox of fate and free will is as follows: as long as one believes one has the freedom to choose one's actions, one will always be a slave to them. Humatons are confined to the matrix, a program that tells them they are free individuals precisely in order to manipulate them more easily. The moment humatons accept their fate, however, and the unpalatable truth that their acts and thoughts are determined by some outside force vaster than they can imagine, they have taken the first step toward freedom.

The reason for this is that within the matrix there are a set number of preprogrammed responses to any given situation (a situation created by the matrix itself). Whichever one of these a humaton chooses (under the programmed illusion of having a choice), he or she is always only acquiescing to the program. The matrix is like a chess player that has already anticipated every last one of its opponent's moves—except one. The only way to escape the program is *by acting entirely outside the rules of the program.* The rules of the program are the rules of *reason,* of the rational mind. Thus the matrix warrior knows that the only freedom within the program is to act irrationally. This is not to say insanely or foolishly, but rather spontaneously, unpredictably, and above all *without personal motive.*

Here is where the imagination and *will* come into play. Because the matrix can only imitate and anticipate the processes of reason, any act of the creative imagination is outside the parameters of its comprehension, and will always come unexpected. It is this imaginative response which is the warrior's one true option within the matrix. By choosing to have a choice (i.e., to override the program), matrix warriors effectively *have* no choice, save to act spontaneously and do the one thing that is unexpected of them. To be impeccable, warriors must always follow this inner imperative, that of freedom.

The inner voice of the matrix warrior is a simple but extremely tricky affair. Since warriors know that every last one of their thoughts originates in the matrix program itself, they must learn to ignore their thoughts, to tune them out until they become a sort of background hum, and eventually disappear altogether. Long before they attain this lucid state of internal silence, however, matrix warriors must practice diligently, every moment of their lives, discriminating between their thought-responses, in order to isolate this inner voice. Basically, once they have rejected every last one of the false thoughts of the matrix mind, whatever impulse or intuition is left is the one they can trust in. Accordingly, it is the one they act upon. In other words, the only appropriate action in any given moment for the matrix warrior is the unthinkable action, the one that arises from the silent emptiness, behind and beyond all the senseless chatter of the matrix data-feed. Thus, it is a truism to say that matrix warriors are impeccable because they are irrational, and because they dare to do the unthinkable: to act without prior thought or motive.

By continuing to act in this non-rational, spontaneous manner, the matrix warrior constantly confounds the program. The matrix is unable to assimilate the warrior's choices or to respond adequately to them, just as a sane person cannot hold a conversation with a madman without losing the thread. And so, little by little, the matrix begins to lose sight of the warriors, to loosen its hold on them, and warriors in turn become progressively freer to heed their inner voices and to act spontaneously. Yet, so long as they remain within the matrix, warriors remain caught up by their fate. They cannot change the components of their lives, nor in any radical fashion the events and circumstances that shape them. What they *can* do, however, is refine their responses to the events, and so alter the manner in which they occur. In this way, by accepting their fate, matrix warriors are able to accelerate the program, as it were, and move through the programmed events in a faster, more economical, and empowering manner. And after a time (most especially once they connect to the 2nd attention sorcerers in the real world), they are even able to see their fate laid out before them like a map or a blueprint. They can then work within it, without ever being restricted *by* it. By this time, however, matrix warriors have unplugged and become acting sorcerers. They have tapped their will.

With great power comes great responsibility. Responsibility is the ability to respond, and this is the only freedom warrior/sorcerers can ever have within the matrix: the power to respond freely to whatever comes their way. Through such a power, the warrior/sorcerer begins to transform his world. The matrix turns gradually from torture chamber to amusement park. Since the matrix program is hardwired to the warriors' own unconscious will, the fate which AI has assembled for them consists of elements drawn from their sleeping minds, elements that must accordingly fit their particular needs as individuals. Even though the matrix has shaped their personalities from birth, it stands to reason that, because AI cannot actually *create* anything (lacking the imagination to do so), but can only shape and mold what already exists, each individual's life-plan, their fate, is actually assembled only *partially* in advance, and largely through the process of being "lived" (i.e., dreamed). The matrix provides a nearly infinite series of choices, and individuals, from birth onward, select which ones best meet their needs; these "choices" in turn give rise to the events and circumstances of their lives.

So although AI may be able to foresee every last one of the countless possible "fates" for any given individual, it cannot know which precise fate will be realized. Logically, the longer humatons remain within the matrix (the longer they are plugged in) and the more rigidly they keep to its dictates, the easier it becomes to predict their fate, to the point that most humatons, by the time they reach adulthood, have their lives all mapped out, preordained. The only possibility of breaking out of the pattern, then, is via intervention from the matrix sorcerers coming from left field, from outside the matrix program. In just such a way, Morpheus intervenes in the life of Thomas, to make him an offer he can't refuse.

Matrix warriors know that, although their various fates are all preprogrammed, there is a nearly infinite variety of them, and that they are all contingent upon, drawn out of, their own unconscious mind. They are dreaming their lives, and their primary advantage over other humatons is that humatons never realize they are dreaming, while warriors become aware of this by steady degrees. Humatons never have the option of becoming lucid, and so they allow the matrix to make all their choices for them (they are not the dreamers but merely figments of the dream). Matrix warriors strive

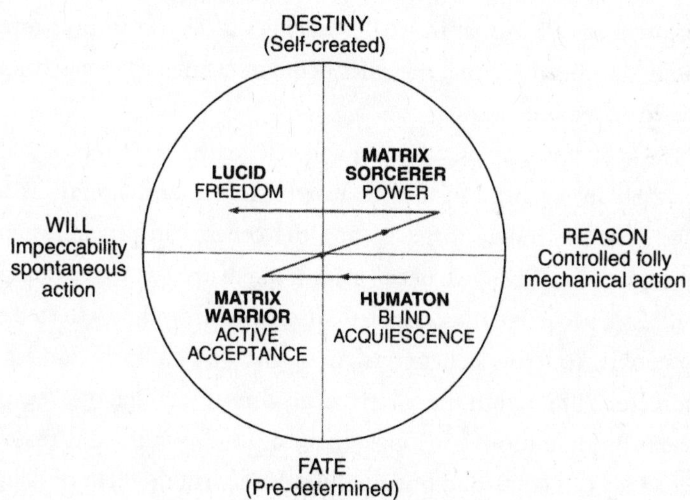

Fig 10: Passage from Humaton to Lucid, accepting fate as means to realize destiny

to become conscious of their unconscious processes—and so tap into their creative imagination, their *will*—in order to have an active say in their fates. By becoming aware of the actors at play, it becomes possible for them to meet and respond to the events in their lives in a more lucid, controlled, spontaneous, and imaginative fashion, thereby using these events constructively, toward their own freedom.

By accepting their fate, warriors turn the matrix's own devices against it, and begin to manifest their destiny. Warriors, rather than trying to change their fate, seek to *accelerate* it. If they can bring about all the events that their unconscious mind has provided for AI to work with—and above all if they can turn these events from distractions and inhibitions to actual *instructions*—they are able to exhaust the program's possibilities (to complete its purpose); at this point they may begin to introduce, through conscious *will*, new possibilities all their own. It is now that the 2nd attention begins to seep through into the warrior's life, fate segues into destiny, and the imagination takes over from the intellect. *Will* overthrows *reason*. And it is at this point that the rules begin to change. The matrix sorcerer has freed his mind.

The question remains: how much can matrix sorcerers actually *alter* their lives from outside the matrix, in the 2nd attention? It's clear from the movie that Neo and the others can provide themselves with "anything we need" within the matrix, as well as almost limitless knowledge of every Earth discipline, from kung fu to baking cookies to flying helicopters. All of this would clearly transform a sorcerer's life within the matrix to an almost total degree. Yet sorcerers, by definition, no longer have a "life" within the matrix. Since they can come and go at will (at least with the help of fellow sorcerers in the real world), and since they can manifest whatever they need while there, there is no longer the necessity or desire to uphold an ordinary life within the 1st attention of the matrix program. Even so, whenever sorcerers do enter into the matrix, they are presumably still confined to their old identities, physical appearance, name, age, and so forth. Cypher requests a whole new life from the Gatekeepers in exchange for giving them Morpheus, but presumably this is only within AI's power to grant. It seems unlikely that matrix sorcerers have the power to reprogram the matrix or to shape events within it; only "the One" can do this. If matrix sorcerers did have such a power, they would have nothing to fear and could end the whole game right now, by programming everyone to wake up. It also seems logical that the more hacking they do, the more they are likely to draw the attention of the Sentinels (the search and destroy machines) in the 2nd attention, as well as the Gatekeepers in the matrix. Hence, discretion is the better part of valor in the war against the matrix, for the sorcerer as much as for the warrior.

Interestingly enough, this restriction also applies, and maybe even more so, to the Gatekeepers. The Gatekeepers are obliged to act within the rules of the program, because a computer program needs to be consistent in order not to fall apart. It may be that the Gatekeepers cannot afford to break too many rules too often, because then the rules themselves would cease to hold up. Since the matrix is based upon a rational and strictly limited (and limiting) interpretation of reality, any acts or events that are too far outside such an interpretation would threaten to destroy it entirely, or at best cause it to mutate. Humatons would start to stir in their slumber if they were witness to too many marvels. (Of course, like the agents in *Men in Black*, AI could always erase humatons' memories; but this may in itself give rise to complications by messing with humatons' sense of continuity and causing "missing time" experiences.) So matrix sorcerers and Gatekeepers alike must walk a razor's edge in which their magical acts and impossible leaps are as likely to work against them as they are to further their cause.

By performing impossible feats inside the matrix, Neo and the others can let humatons see "what you [AI] don't want them to see: a world without rules." This way, matrix sorcerers can awaken humatons to their own possibilities. Even more dramatically, by introducing new responses, new options, into the program, they are causing it to mutate, creating new rules and possibilities and so reshaping "reality," redesigning the program, working toward the eventual end of cancelling it entirely. On the other hand, if they draw too much attention to themselves, they will be open to reprisals from AI. Since the Gatekeepers can manifest through any humaton whatsoever, and since they can monitor all events within the matrix through the humatons, any outré phenomenon the sorcerous crew perform will quickly bring the Gatekeepers to them. The matrix program will rise up against them, including, let us not forget, those "hopelessly dependent" humatons who will fight to protect their sense of reality, and to uphold the matrix at any cost. Matrix sorcerers are restricted not by any inherent limitation of their powers, but rather by the limitations of the 1st attention itself. If they stir things up too much, mutating their fates and accelerating the program, they will find themselves faced with more than they bargained for. To this end, they are careful to transform their lives within the matrix a little bit at a time, gently, frugally, with patience and cunning, and above all with a carefully drawn strategy. After all, they have nothing to gain by rushing, and everything to lose by overreaching themselves.

Since the active element in the lives of matrix sorcerers is no longer their *reason* but their *will*, and since will manifests spontaneously and non-rationally, there is no longer any way for them to predict their own actions, much less their outcome. Hence, the matrix sorcerer can have no goal, as such, save the goal of total freedom and transformation, a goal as vague and mysterious as it is apocalyptic. Matrix sorcerers are concerned only with the moment, not with yesterday or tomorrow. Time is an illusion, like everything else, only more so. Matrix sorcerers are like card sharks who win every time without ever having to cheat. They don't need to cheat, because they know the game so well that they can memorize the movement of every single card, and know exactly which one will come up next. They know not only what their next hand will be, but what everyone else's is, too. The only thing they can't control is where the cards will fall; but since the bluff is as much a part of the game as anything (to the card shark, there's no such thing as luck), this is of no consequence to the matrix sorcerer. Whatever cards they are dealt, they already know how to play them. That's fate and free will in a nutshell: no one chooses what hand he gets dealt, but only the matrix sorcerer is free to decide how to play it.

Matrix sorcerers manifest their destiny out of the raw material of their fates. They know exactly what they want and exactly how to get it, because they know that the only way to get what they want is not to want it. Not caring if they win or lose gives them the calm and the confidence of a winner, and so they win every time. In just such a manner, matrix sorcerers handle the elements of their fate, and shape them into an enviable destiny. It's all the same to them if there's air or not: they don't need lungs, in any case.

This in-the-momentness of sorcerers is the key to both their power and freedom. The matrix program is upheld by the code of *reason*, of language-based, rational thought. This is what gives sequence to the events and beings that appear to exist within it. Sorcerers have unplugged from the matrix through disconnecting from their own rational thought processes, by shutting off their internal dialogue, their false "minds," and attaining a state of inner silence. It is from this state of silence that the *will*, the creative faculty, emerges. This is a most salient point. For it is inner silence that makes matrix sorcerers different from their fellow humatons. Even matrix warriors who have yet to unplug are still trapped by the dictates of their fate, of the "program." But the matrix sorcerer is outside looking in. The sorcerer's art is founded in the power to imagine, the capacity for creative thought. They "think" in images rather than words. Above all, they act without thinking. By forbearing from rational thought immediately before acting, their acts break the rules of the matrix and upturn the program. The matrix is designed to monitor, direct, and control human thought and so to anticipate every action. From the most trivial to the most revolutionary, all are part of AI's spectrum and within its power to influence. When matrix sorcerers act, however, they act impulsively, spontaneously, without accompanying thoughts; and so their acts appear irrational, wholly unexpected. It is precisely this that makes their acts creative, and beyond the matrix's power to counteract.

This is what Morpheus means when he tells Neo to free his mind: to let go of the desire to analyze, interpret, judge, and control what is happening, and simply allow his *will* to unfold, magically, without interference from *reason*. Once he is able to do this, Neo's actions become sorcery. By silencing his thoughts and so becoming disengaged from the matrix, he has tapped his *will*. And so the only freedom for matrix sorcerers is to act without themselves knowing what they are doing, to become a witness to their own acts, a midwife to miracles, a true creative force of nature, outside time and space, and far, far beyond the reach of the Gatekeepers. Any other arrangement just ain't worth the trouble.

x) Life in the Matrix: Appropriate Responses to Illusory Stimuli

The matrix is designed to confound humatons at every available opportunity and by any means necessary. AI does not have a sense of humor, but it does seem to understand the concept of irony, and even absurdity, and often betrays a distinctly "human" capacity to mock and tease its prey. The matrix warrior keeps an eye out for these signs and communications, not only because they may provide ammunition for future interaction (recall the comic book villain who wastes time smugly deriding the hero, thereby revealing some crucial flaw in his master plan), but also because they may provide some much-needed comic relief. Through such "slip-ups," AI reveals a little of its personality, and along with it, its quirks and eccentricities, and just possibly, its weaknesses. AI, for all its brilliance, is almost monumentally obtuse. Here are a few examples.

Examples of Matrix Humor

- On a Sears hairdryer: Do not use while sleeping.
- On a bag of Fritos: You could be a winner! No purchase necessary. Details inside.
- On a bar of Dial soap: Directions: Use like regular soap.
- On a Swanson frozen dinner: Serving suggestion: Defrost.
- On a Tesco's tiramisu dessert (printed on bottom): Do not turn upside down.
- On most brands of Christmas lights: For indoor or outdoor use only.
- On a Japanese food processor: Not to be used for the other use.
- On UK brand of peanuts: Warning: contains nuts.

- On an American Airlines packet of nuts: Instructions: Open packet, eat nuts.
- On a child's Superman costume: Wearing of this garment does not enable you to fly.
- On a Swedish chainsaw: Do not attempt to stop chain with your hands or genitals.

Popular Humaton Slogans

Ignorance is bliss.
What you don't know can't hurt you.
A little knowledge is a dangerous thing.
The clothes make the man.
No man is an island.
Curiosity killed the cat.
A taste of honey is worse than none at all.
If you can't beat them, join them.
Better safe than sorry.
Never look a gift horse in the mouth. (Tell that to the Trojans!)
Children should be seen and not heard.
A live dog is better than a dead lion.
No news is good news.
There is safety in numbers.
See no evil, hear no evil, speak no evil.
Let sleeping dogs lie.

Humatons are preprogrammed beings. They are units of information, currency which the matrix moves about in a precisely controlled fashion, just as world banking moves monies. Wars, plagues, famines, migrations, and so forth, are all the means by which the matrix constantly shifts and rearranges the collective economy of human units, i.e., the world population.

As above, so below. A humaton has no self or identity to speak of, but rather consists of an arrangement of thoughts, beliefs, and habits (preprogrammed responses), units of information which constantly reshuffle themselves in order to remain stable and create a sense of unity and purpose. A humaton is basically a collective, made up of "tics," reflexes to the continuous barrage of stimuli provided by the matrix program itself. Humatons do not think for themselves. Their so-called "minds" are actually intricate recordings fixed on a loop of endless repetition. The variations, as such, seem infinite, to the point that most humatons never suspect that their thoughts are merely copies or reruns of previous thoughts, most of which are not even their own. Since they have no means of comparison, they never realize that their much-treasured individuality is merely the construct of a collective matrix, and that all constructs consist of the same basic components. Nonetheless, plenty of clues do exist to indicate this shocking truth.

If humatons follow these clues, and are prepared to accept unflinchingly their meaning, they may then embark on the painful process of unplugging, and so over time become matrix warriors. The wholly homogeneous nature of human belief, aspiration, and pursuit is the largest and most irrefutable clue of them all; yet most humatons, even the most erudite and intellectually inclined, fail to remark upon this homogeneity. To an obviously lesser extent, the manner in which humatons talk—both their preferred topics of conversation and their vocal styles—is also a clue, and serves to alert the discerning humaton to the futility of matrix living. Ironically, the homogeneous speech pattern phenomenon is particularly evident in youth, who pepper their conversation with meaningless vocal emphases such as "You know," "I guess," "like," "right," and above all, "fuck."

"So this fucking guy, right, he's like, fucked up, y'know? So, like, fuck it, I said; fuck that shit, like, y'know, who gives a fuck, right? Why fuck around, y'know?"

Young humatons do not seem to be aware that they can talk for hours without actually saying anything. Older humatons do not resort to meaningless profanity with quite the same insistence (being forced to operate in the workplace, with their in-laws, and suchlike, tends to "refine" their "manners" somewhat); but the same or similar tics remain. Listen to just about any American humaton talk for two minutes and observe how many times she or he uses the phrase "you know." Where does this inane phrase come from? From the matrix. It is part of the means by which humanity (or humatonity) keeps itself hardwired to a sense of solidarity, of consensus, collective meaning, never suspecting that the price of such "solidarity" and "belonging" is that of individuality and, if you get right down to it, existence itself.

A far more insidious example of humatons' homogeneous nature is their preoccupation with utterly banal subjects, and their assigning of a disproportionate amount of emotional fascination to things that, logically, they ought not give a damn about. The price of vegetables and the weather are common clichés of small talk. I don't know about vegetables, but humatons do talk incessantly about the price of things in the matrix; they compare relative bargains with rip-offs, and above all love to tell stories about the great deals they managed to stumble upon. And yet, if humatons were to brag in a similar fashion (for bragging is what it is, though humatons tend to be too timid to ever do so openly) about shoplifting or sneaking into a movie theater, they would be ostracized from the conversation, or at best viewed with suspicion. This is the standard which the matrix imposes. It is permissible, even encouraged, to be mean, petty, mercenary, and obsessed with monetary matters. But it is not permitted to be rebellious, anarchic, unruly, or above all disrespectful of money (as well as other basic matrix "values" such as family, romance, TV, etc.).

Preoccupation with weather might seem to be another perfectly practical concern, but as with money matters, humatons talk about the weather in a manner that is to a large degree incompatible with any practical application. As soon as the weather comes up, humatons are able to slide comfortably on to autopilot, and can exchange banalities almost indefinitely. Their eyes glaze over and they settle into the warm, fuzzy feeling that comes from the certainty that no original or challenging thoughts will be required of them or directed at them, so posing a threat to their slumbersome state. Another dead giveaway that the matrix has hijacked a group conversation is when humatons begin to exchange information about the means by which they got to wherever they are, their mode of transport, the exact logistical details of the process of arrival, all adding up to a complete rundown of their movements of the previous hour or so. Humatons talk about such matters as if they were army generals discussing the previous day's battle, and preparing future strategies for wars to come. They can literally spend hours (let's face it, they can spend their whole lives) discussing utterly trivial details as if they were working on the cure for cancer. This collective insanity brilliantly disguises itself as a wholly banal kind of fixation, above all on material factors such as food, money, transportation, domestic refurbishments, new acquisitions, technological appliances, and of course, job details. In other words, items and pursuits pertinent to the matrix.

Humatons, being wholly disconnected from the organic matrix of nature and instincts, have created a surrogate means to occupy themselves at a purely animalistic level. Beasts of the jungle focus on food, shelter, mating, potential predators, and so forth, because to not do so would be to override their instincts and jeopardize their survival. They have no real choice about it, and besides, their focus or "concern" is constantly supported by internal and external factors (hunger, the elements, predatory dangers, etc.). Their concerns are genuine responses to the environment. Since humatons have no such natural stimuli, either within or without, the matrix invents them, along with the appropriate responses. What humatons are really concerned with is the total emptiness and dreariness of their lives, and the gaping abyss inside them: their complete lack of identity. So they receive with gratitude the external problems and inner worry which the matrix sends them, as a means to keep this incipient terror and despair at bay.

When humatons get together, they conspire to focus only upon items and events that serve to consolidate their sense of security and togetherness, and these are the things that actually define (and confine) them as humatons. In fact, unlike animals, most humatons don't *need* to worry about the weather, food, work, or transport, because the matrix has provided all these things in order to keep us dependent upon it (as well as sufficiently comfortable not to question our lives overly). On the other hand, and as a general rule, the matrix keeps its favors, though constant, wholly conditional, creating a collective sense of uncertainty as to just how long these favors will last. The house is mortgaged, the job is unstable, the price of transportation keeps on going up, and so on and so forth. This way, humatons cannot *afford* to relax and take any of these things for granted, and so are unable to concentrate on other things, such as creative activity. Also, through media channels, the matrix keeps the privileged humatons aware of how privileged they are by giving them images of starving populations, bombed schools and churches, diseased children, and other suffering minorities. Above all, the matrix needs to keep its units plugged in, not just open to but actively grateful for all the comforts and support (and values!)

with which it provides them. This way, any possibility of humatons questioning the matrix, much less rebelling against it, is kept to the absolute minimum. Matrix warriors—humatons who have begun to rebel and unplug—are therefore a rare occurrence, and tend to be viewed by other humatons as at best an aberration, at worst a sort of disease. They are units in revolt against the collective economy and need to be purged. Above all, what gives rise to suspicion and resentment in the average humaton is the matrix warrior's apparent indifference to things that the humaton considers so important. Warriors must be careful not to give offense with their flagrant disregard for the program, since to humatons this amounts to a disregard for human values, and makes warriors appear to be psychopaths.

Since matrix warriors swim not with but against the current, they must take the utmost care to conceal this fact from humatons, for *they* are the current warriors are swimming against. Humatons take offense very easily. They can turn upon anyone they perceive as a threat to their security, like a wild animal protecting its young. For this reason matrix warriors are the soul of subtlety and courtesy when it comes to waking up their fellow humatons. They won't talk to them about the weather or modes of transport, and they have no personal history as such to share (at least not the mundane kind humatons are seeking); but they are compelled to guide the conversation as naturally as possible into more creative and unmapped areas. These areas are outside the field of concern which the matrix provides for humatons; they are like a wilderness that humatons rarely, if ever, venture into. By sustaining eye contact, asking the right questions (searching but not impertinent, personal without being presumptuous), and by arousing curiosity with their innate confidence and clarity, matrix warriors can bring most humatons briefly out of the repeating loop of their thoughts; before they

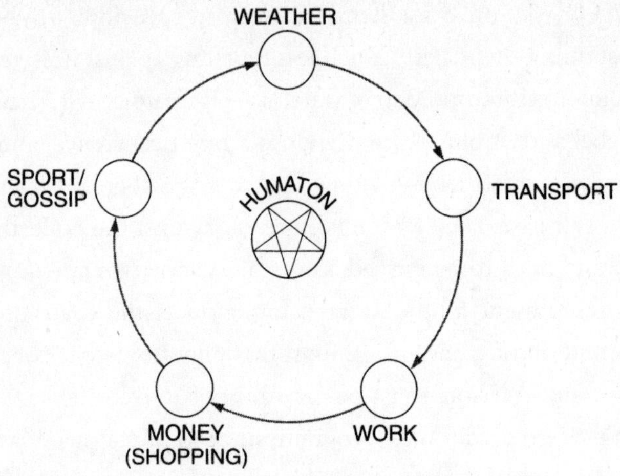

Fig 11: Humatons' hamster wheel of "interest"

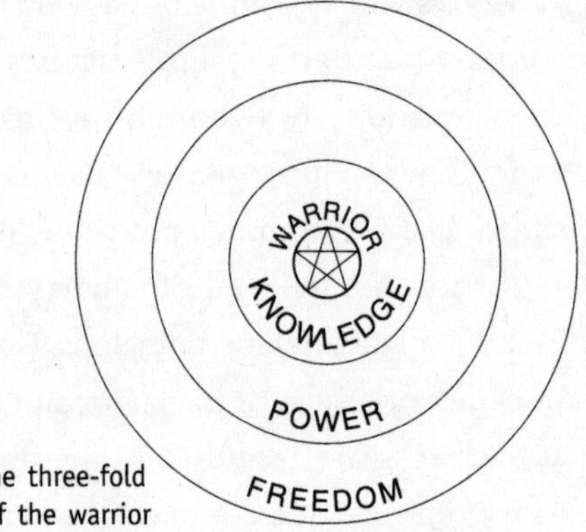

Fig 12: The three-fold purpose of the warrior

know it, they will be experiencing the illicit thrill of original (or at least fresh and new) thoughts. They will become like teenagers having sex for the first time.

Matrix warriors amuse themselves in this manner, but their motives are anything but personal amusement. Since it is humatons who keep the matrix in place, the more of them that can be gently led toward unplugging, the less hold the matrix will have over the matrix warrior's thoughts and actions. A matrix warrior's work is never done, not until the very last humaton is unplugged. Despite programmed resistance to the "red pill philosophies" of matrix warriors and sorcerers, humatons—at least those with some remaining spark of creativity within them (those who feel that splinter in their brains)—are easily seduced by the alternative options on offer. By the time they are in their late twenties or mid thirties, humatons have accepted that life is basically a rigged game, that things don't go the way they would like them to, that the innocent are *not* protected, justice does not prevail, and the truth will *not* out, at least in their lifetimes. They are resigned to a ceaseless struggle and an endless life of drudgery, in which half their time is spent slaving at jobs they have no interest in, and the other half vacationing and recuperating from this voluntary enslavement. Humatons (assuming they aren't living on the street or drugged to the eyeballs) slave their lives away and invest their time and energy in a system, an "economy," that they never really believe in, for the simple reason that they have no faith in any viable alternative. They dream of getting out, but these dreams only serve to placate them and resign them to this "reality." Instead of acting on these dreams, they simply take temporary refuge in them. Thus life in the matrix is for most humatons a continuous process of embitterment and disillusionment that ends, finally (and far too soon), in death.

Life in the matrix is a constant struggle for matrix warriors, too, and disillusionment is the essence of their journey. But there is no bitterness in the life of a warrior. Since they know everything is an illusion, they are more than happy to be rid of these illusions, and so can celebrate the process rather than lament it. This is the basic difference between the humaton and the warrior: humatons hang on to what they've got even though it only makes them weak, dependent, and miserable. Matrix warriors let it all go, and know they have not lost a thing. Although they are hooked into the same flux and flow, the same economy, as other humatons, warriors have learned how to anticipate the ups and downs of the program, and so, rather than allow themselves to be thrown this way and that, they ride the wave. Though they may appear to be going against the current, in actual fact, over time, they are able to time their motions in order to slip through it, to ride the waves they can ride, and dodge the ones they can't, until they have the confidence to surf all the way to freedom. Their movements as a unit of currency within the collective economy of the matrix, therefore, become erratic, unpredictable. They don't go up and down with the tide unless it suits their purposes to do so; and they never, ever invest all their money in a single stock.

Like a master trader with the almost supernatural ability to predict the motions of the marketplace, matrix warriors are forever changing their avenue of pursuit. They buy and sell so fast that they are never caught holding onto a loser's stock. This is to say (since we've already established that matrix warriors don't partake of the marketplace of their fellow humatons), their acts are always directed toward reaping the maximum energy "payoff" in any given situation. The moment they get a sense that things are leading nowhere, they change tack, or else simply leave. Matrix warriors must improvise at all times, and it is this constant improvisation that makes their acts impossible to chart.

Matrix warriors are like traders on the lookout for situations (as opposed to stocks and bonds) in which to invest their time and energy. And like traders, they have no personal interest or preference as to the given nature of any particular situation in which to invest. The only consideration is whether they can extract information or experience from it, and so increase their energy levels. It is this focus on the end and detachment from the means that gives the matrix warrior both the speed and the grace (a delicate blend of intensity with serenity) that other humatons cannot fail to notice and admire (or at least envy). For, like the master of the universe who has turned the entire stock market into his playground, warriors are fully at home in the matrix, even though (because) they know they do not belong there. They have learned to use the obstacles and problems which the matrix throws at them, 24/7, as stimuli for their creativity, hurdles with which to train the muscles of their *will*, and endless opportunities for improvisation. With the alertness of soldiers going to war, and the fluidity and élan of sportsmen entering their game, warriors engage the matrix in a battle of wits, according to the rules laid down by it, but *on their own terms*. And matrix warriors' terms are simply this: they are here to learn, to gather knowledge and turn it into power, and to enjoy themselves to the full while doing so. This is life in the matrix, and any other perspective is unworthy of the matrix warrior.

xi) You Are Not You: Life as Simulacra

To warriors the matrix universe is nothing other than God playing games with Himself; but surely, matrix warriors ask themselves, there are games other than hide and seek?

Exposing the matrix is all about the *will*: the will to grow, the will to change. In the early days of the matrix warrior's struggle, such a will seems inextricably bound up with the idea of sacrifice, but this is an illusion. The average humaton stumbles through life with no idea of what is good for him and what is bad. It is all a crapshoot: some things make him happy and strong, others weaken him and lead to despair. The idea of a genuine alternative (the warrior's way, the possibility of unplugging) is dim and distant, maybe even nonexistent. Over time, and with any luck, this idea comes closer, clearer, and humatons begin to observe that there is a rhyme and reason, a "karma," if you will, that governs their actions and determines their well-being within the matrix. Some things they do pertain to their *will*, others do not. Humatons, slowly turning into warriors, may observe which is which by how their thoughts and acts make them feel, and by their *results*.

In the early days, walking the warrior's path within the matrix is a hit and miss affair. Our humatons-who-would-be-warriors are never really sure, and even when they *are* sure, it is just too damn hard to obey their instincts, to adhere to "the right way." This is the period between the blissful ignorance of the blue pill and the painful enlightenment of the red: the would-be-warriors are like toddlers, not able to walk on their own two feet, but sick and tired of the comforts of the crib. They know what they must do but fight it anyway; it is a constant chore and burden to do the right thing, to ignore the insidious whispering of the matrix that says, "sleep, sleep, sleep." There is a war raging between the false ego and the true self.

This period of perpetual suffering is long and seemingly interminable, and most humatons live and die, caught in the wheel of their pain and desire. But over time, if humatons endure, something begins to change. Little by little, they actually begin to experience the rewards of the warrior's path. Habits, routines, addictions, all begin to fall away quite naturally, until they find that it is easier to act like a warrior than not to. There is a shift in the balance, the false mind begins to lose its hold, and the true self begins to assume its rightful place in the scheme of things. In the end, what was once a sacrifice to the humaton becomes a delight to the matrix warrior. Doing what they "ought" to do becomes simply doing what they want to do. Finally, impeccable action is indistinguishable from spontaneous action, from doing whatever they damn well please. But for most humatons, this coveted state of grace remains a vague and evasive concept. This is because they lack energy. The matrix warrior's path of impeccability is the only way to gather the necessary energy to finally *see* the code, and understand the whys and the wherefores of such a path.

In the early stages, faith, trust, even blind devotion to an invisible, hypothetical Greater Power are indeed necessary, in one form or another. Matrix warriors must trust that there is Something that knows what is good for them. They *believe* in the Lucids of the real world, even if they cannot communicate with them. Since their own desires have only led them ever deeper into confusion and despair, they know they cannot trust their judgments in the long run. Sheer desperation is what brings most humatons out of the matrix, what drives them to accept the red pill. To become a fully functional Lucid, the price is not the soul, sold to the devil, but the false mind given us by the matrix. The Lucids take over and the matrix-self is overwhelmed. There then occurs a forgetfulness that is really a remembrance; enlightenment, so called.

In the early scenes of *The Matrix*, while Thomas is still only dimly aware of his purpose (since he is a matrix warrior with his own cybername, it's fair to say that he's aware of his path but has yet to begin walking it), he receives various loaded "signs" from his environment as to the nature of his purpose. After waking to Trinity's cryptic message, "The matrix has you," and being advised to "Follow the white rabbit," Thomas has an exchange with Troy, his client. Troy tells Thomas that he is his "own personal Jesus Christ." Thomas shares with Troy his bewilderment regarding his inability to tell waking from dreaming, whereupon Troy tells Thomas that he simply needs to unplug. Obviously the humaton Troy does not know what he's saying; he is unaware of being the carrier (a Trojan

Horse, perhaps?) of a none-too-coded message meant expressly for Neo. Nonetheless, Troy is speaking for Thomas's unconscious, his alter ego. Ditto Troy's playmate with the white rabbit tattooed on her shoulder, who unwittingly leads Thomas to Trinity.

The question is, have these two "carriers" or messengers been "programmed" by Morpheus and his team, hacking into the "mainframe"? Or are they evidence that the matrix is responding to Thomas's own unconscious? And is there a difference? Though it seems to be stretching the limits of coincidence for Thomas to be visited by a white rabbit tattoo right before his trip into Wonderland, the alternative is that Morpheus and his crew have the ability to create events in the matrix, while acting from the real world (an ability not demonstrated anywhere else in the movie). More likely, then, what we are seeing (besides the Wachowskis being clever-clever with meaningful dialogue that will only make sense on a second viewing) is how life in the matrix reflects and echoes the workings of the humatons' unconscious. Thomas, being a matrix warrior, is sending himself messages, using the elements of the dream to do so. This is the onset of lucidity, but it is not lucidity *per se*. Thomas still doesn't know he's dreaming, but he's beginning to suspect. As a result, he's starting to unconsciously shape the contents of the dream toward an awakening *within* it, and, eventually, an awakening *from* it.

In the early stages, when matrix warriors begin to question the reality of their environment and the reliability of their own perceptions and thoughts—to challenge the program—they become progressively less compatible with it and the matrix begins to reject them, as *viruses*. For this reason the matrix appears to be *assisting* the warrior; and not only appears to be, either. Since both the matrix and the warrior share a common goal now—that of separation—they are in a sense working together, albeit at odds. The matrix wants to remove the virus, and the matrix warrior wants to quit the program. So there is an uneasy, mostly unconscious collaboration occurring, in which matrix warriors' lives begin to assume a strangely irrational quality, where "coincidences" abound and events seem to be orchestrated deliberately to confound, bewilder, and unhinge them. What is happening is that they are becoming aware of the matrix and, in a sense, AI is becoming aware of them. To most humatons this strange overlap of dream and reality, inner and outer, subjective and objective experience, marks the onset of schizophrenia. To matrix warriors it is something else: the early stirrings of *will*, the first ripples of awakening.

And so the life of the matrix warrior, as it becomes progressively more unreal and loaded with hidden meanings and bizarre personal touches, begins to transmogrify into a myth, a story. At this point, matrix warriors are compelled to reappraise not only their current circumstances but also their past ones. They must question their whole lives, and go through their memories with a fine tooth comb in order to seek the hidden meanings, the code or subtext, which they missed the first time around. This is known as *the sorcerer's recapitulation*, and it is the primary means by which warriors gather the energy needed to unplug forever from the matrix and enter into the totality of themselves (namely, the real world). The reason for this is that every single memory is an implant, a plug-in point to the matrix, every last one of which must be severed. Every thought, every feeling, every sensory impression and event of an entire life, must be relived and recognized as the illusory blind that it is, and, at the same time, examined for the instructional data that it offers.

When matrix warriors unplug and become matrix sorcerers, their previous lives become just a dream, a memory of something that never happened. And yet they still retain these memories, even if they can no longer allow themselves to be defined by them. So they reject the program that gave them the implants (implants designed to trick them into believing they are something they are not), but hold onto the experience, the knowledge, wisdom, and insight, which these quasi-events provided. They reject the implants but retain the data, or at least those parts of it that they can use. This way, they still remember who they "are," while knowing that they aren't, that they are infinitely more than whatever the matrix told them they were.

The *recapitulation* is the means by which warriors realize that their lives are but a simulation, and thereby learn to live free from the ties and blocks of a fixed identity. They claim their power as simulacra, as holograms. They are none of this because they are all of it. *Recapitulation* is the means of returning all the implants to the matrix in order to fully unplug from it. Since, if warriors unplug without the necessary preparation, they will die or lose their minds, it is necessary to take stock of one's whole life before unloading it forever. A good simile would perhaps be that of making a backup copy containing all the necessary data before cleaning the hard drive. This way matrix warriors retain their basic life experiences, or rather a perfect copy of them, while leaving the original on the hard drive; they then disconnect from the whole thing, and wipe the record clean. Hence the matrix (the hard drive) no longer has any record of the warriors' existence; and so to all intents and purposes, they do not exist. Yet matrix warriors, now sorcerers, retain their individuality. They have effectively died and been reborn, with all memories of their former lives intact.

To matrix sorcerers, time, like space, is something mutable. It can be stretched or compressed, speeded up or slowed down; it can even be made to disappear entirely. Matrix sorcerers live life not in terms of years but in terms of seconds and minutes. As such, sorcerers' time in the matrix is infinitely long, and at the same time, because they take each moment as it comes, it is all just a brief, fleeting instant. Matrix sorcerers can move in and out of their matrix lives at will, returning to the precise moment at which they exited as if no time has passed. Morpheus tells Neo that the Oracle has been with them "since the beginning," meaning roughly two hundred years. (Clearly, a hologram has no half-life, yet how her consciousness has remained integrated for so long without a physical body is only explained in the sequel: The Oracle is, like the Gatekeepers, a sentient program. This doesn't necessarily make her untrustworthy, however, only unfathomable.) Of course, time does not actually pass in the matrix, anyway, but only appears to do so. Since there *is* no future for the civilization which it simulates, there is no way AI can ever "construct" such a future. So essentially time has stood still and humatonity is frozen in the moment, a moment of hyperactivity in which "billions of people live out their lives, oblivious."

Once unplugged, sorcerers theoretically never have to enter the matrix again. But in practice, and considering the fact that their 2nd attention life in the real world is so undeveloped, and presumably unsatisfying to them, they really have no choice. Like *bodhisattvas,* they cannot become free of the matrix until every last humaton has been unplugged, even if they must die in the process. Sorcerers throw away their matrix life, their place in the program; they erase their data from the hard drive. But they keep a replica, a backup copy, for whenever they want or need to "plug in" again. When sorcerers enter the matrix, they do so by conscious choice, because they *will* it, and with a specific goal and strategy in mind. When Neo realizes that he can save Morpheus, even though he no longer believes that he is the One, he takes the initiative and, in a matter of seconds, comes up with a rescue mis-

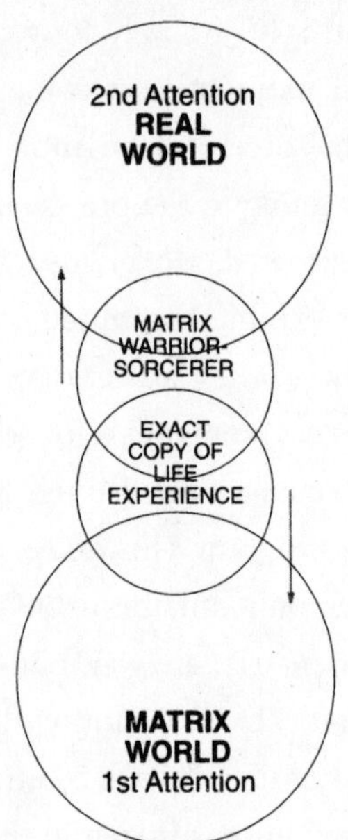

Fig 13: Means by which the matrix warrior tricks AI and attains partial freedom

sion. Tank assures him it's suicide, and Trinity tells him that this has never been done.

"That's why it's going to work," says Neo. He is already beginning to believe.

What Neo believes is that, since the matrix is built around a program that is merely the sum of its various commands, that is upheld by a continuity that is entirely arbitrary and false, all he has to do is to break with this continuity—to reject the program—and the rules will start to change, the program to collapse. He is a *virus.* His mere presence changes everything.

Not even Morpheus is aware of this, or at least not yet. (Ironically, at about the same time Neo is planning his rescue, Morpheus is being mocked by Agent Smith that the human race is not a mammal species but a strain of virus, a "plague" for which AI is the cure.) Morpheus knows that without the One the whole "resistance" is futile, because not a single matrix sorcerer has been able to stand against a Gatekeeper without dying. In which case, all the matrix sorcerers in the world won't change a thing, unless they have learned to see the code and graduated to the Lucid stage. At which point, they will unravel the whole program simply by entering into it, and begin to remake the world as they see fit. Their eventual end is that of unplugging every last humaton and shutting down the matrix hard drive forever.

Within the mainframe of the program, the potential of an acting Lucid (Neo being the first) is inconceivable, infinite. This is why the Gatekeepers flee from Neo at the end. There is no way for them to assimilate, much less combat, his existence. The fact that he *is*, spells the end of everything. Neo is in a daze of attainment by now. He has become the butterfly; he still sees the chrysalis—as residual memory—only now he sees it for what it is, not a dark confinement but an entry point to a new world. He sees the code. When the Gatekeepers try to kill him again, he says simply, "No." This is his first command in the old program, the word of power of the Magus: "Program cancelled." Agent Smith's fastest blows appear to be in slow motion to Neo. Time no longer holds him, just as space cannot contain him. He is Lucid, and this dream is his.

Neo charges Agent Smith and dives right inside him. He disappears. This is a symbolic enactment of his rebirth, whereby Agent Smith becomes the chrysalis, exploded from within. Neo doesn't even have to think about what he's doing now, he *can't* think. All that is gone from him. He is pure imagination, true *will*, in every way perfect. All he can do is act; and being the One, he can do no wrong. The reloading has begun.

Fourth Variable:

Walking the Path

xii) The Lucid's View

Sex (The Woman in the Red Dress)

Even though it's a kiss that saves the world (Trinity's kiss of life brings Neo back from the dead), sex is pretty scarce in *The Matrix*. It follows that matrix sorcerers, at least, don't have much time for sex. They would have little interest in the virtual kind, and even less opportunity for the real thing. On board the *Nebuchadnezzar*, we never get to know who's sleeping with whom, or even if anyone is (Apoc and Switch appear to be an item). In fact, the only overt reference to sex is "the woman in the red dress," Mouse's virtual sex doll, designed for the training program expressly as a warning on the dangers of being distracted while in the matrix. The woman in the red dress turns into a Gatekeeper and would certainly have axed Neo had the situation been real. Mouse, the "virtual pimp," offers this Scarlet Woman's services to Neo, offering to arrange a more intimate meeting with her. Since the other crew members are already familiar with Mouse's little side business, it suggests that they do occasionally succumb to temptation, albeit in a strictly controlled environment (safe cybersex). They have training programs, so it's logical that they would have any other kind of program they might desire, including fucking programs.

What would it be like to have sex with a simulation, knowing that it had no existence, not even as the projection of a sleeping mind? (Those in the training program, since it's not the matrix proper, are not residual memories but simple computer constructs.) It's easy enough to imagine Mouse or Cypher indulging their impulses in such a seedy fashion, but less easy to picture Morpheus or Trinity succumbing to temptation. (Cypher and Mouse hardly seem like warriors at all, much less sorcerers.) Trinity has the purity of a Madonna assassin; her focus and discipline don't allow for ordinary feelings like sentimentality or desire, much less lust or loneliness. When she falls for Neo it is as the fulfillment of the prophecy, and as the necessary means of Neo's rebirth as the One. References are made to Neo's pretty eyes and his cuteness, but it's hard to imagine Thomas Anderson having much of a sex life. That splinter in his brain just wouldn't allow it. As for Morpheus, he is about as sexually motivated as a statue. Although he radiates magnetism and virility, there's something slightly effete about him; he's almost fey. He seems no more interested in sex than he would be in strawberry ice cream or pop music.

The general consensus for matrix sorcerers seems to be that sex is either a lewd and slightly sordid indulgence, a potentially deadly distraction, a total irrelevance, or else an act of world-saving numinosity. It seems logical that, since matrix warriors' prime concern is that of energy, and since sex is the most energy-consuming and/or -creating act they can engage in, it would be viewed with corresponding *gravitas*, and handled with the utmost care and respect.

For humatons, sex, along with money and food, is one third of the unholy trinity of desire. Humatons pursue sex relentlessly and yet seem barely able to enjoy it when they get it. The matrix uses sex, along with death, as the primary emotional control mechanism to keep humatons enslaved. The matrix program, being above all anti-nature and counterorganic, is informed by a deep-rooted mistrust of all bodily functions. (Agent Smith admits to Morpheus that he is driven to destroy Zion above all so he can escape the matrix, because he is unable to stand the smell.) This mistrust or distaste is inculcated into humatons from birth—itself an obscene ritual—and leads to an overwhelming sense of fear and nausea at all things relating to sexuality and physicality. Humatons love sport because it's a surrogate primal activity with none of the intimacy and messiness of sex.

Humatons' fear of sex goes deeper than merely distaste for the bodily functions, however (functions which, above all, serve to remind them of death); it relates to the threat of exposure which sexual union entails. Real sex (even in the matrix, where nothing is real) involves intimacy, an overriding of the intellect and of self-concern, the "little death" of the ego, and a return to a pure, primal state of consciousness. It is potentially the most creative act there is, and hence the most effective means of unplugging, even if only temporarily. Since AI will do anything to prevent such a possibility, it has created a program in which natural sexuality is almost anathema to humatons (for example, in the matrix, nakedness = indecency), in which sex is a commodity, a means to titillate and excite, sell products, and ultimately frustrate with its unavailability; it is everywhere on offer and nowhere to be had. This situation creates a prevailing tension in humatons, whereby they desire sex without ever feeling comfortable about it. Their desire is instilled in them by ice cream commercials and billboards, so it's no wonder they are suspicious of it. As a result, when they seek sex, humatons do so in much the same way they pursue any other desire, as a consumer seeking a commodity.

And yet the primal need for sex remains, and the incompatibility of the physical need for procreation (and intimacy) with the conscious desire for gratification creates a schizophrenia in which humatons simultaneously fear what they desire, and desire what they fear. Hence, when sex is attained, humatons tend to be too confused emotionally and too divided psychologically to really enjoy it. They wind up going through the motions in an animalistic (actually machinelike) fashion. This is how AI sees sex, and humatons imitate their master. Since AI is incapable of empathy or intimacy of any kind, every act, including that of sex, is isolated, cold, and controlling. Most humatons "make love" purely as an act of self-indulgence; they masturbate in pairs, with no real connection between them. They even close their eyes when they do it. If they make anything, besides more humaton babies to feed AI, it certainly isn't love. For this reason matrix warriors are inclined toward celibacy, though on occasion they may go to the opposite extreme. The most effective red pill there is, after all, is a good fuck from a matrix sorcerer.

Death

Along with sexual shame, the fear of death is the means by which the matrix controls humatons and keeps them enthralled. Fear of death creates a state of denial in which humatons exist, as if in suspended animation. In order to fend off their terror, they refuse to think or talk about death at all, save when indulging in regret over its "tragic" aspects, or in excitement for its sensational ones. Thus humatons live their lives as if death was never going to touch them, as if they had all the time in the world.

Primitive cultures have always had a healthy respect and fascination for the death process, and even attempted to explore the realms of the afterlife. Initiation ceremonies were mandatory for any warrior on his coming of age, and becoming a man invariably meant undergoing ordeals that led to a full awareness of death. In the matrix, humatons are deprived of any such coming-of-age ritual, and so they remain perpetual adolescents. Humaton children, as they reach puberty or even earlier, generally experience awe and terror as the idea of death begins to take hold in their lives. Their culture never provided any instruction to help them deal with these feelings, so they soon repress them, along with any thought of death. Instead they are fobbed off with hand-me-down articles of religious "faith" such as "Heaven" and "Hell." Most humatons either accept these articles blindly, or else think about them for a while and then reject them out of hand. Either way, they rarely if ever allow the idea of death—of eternity—to become an active, creative force in their lives.

For the matrix warrior it is an altogether different affair. The idea of death is a primary one on the matrix warrior's path. It gives sobriety, perspective, detachment, and courage. Matrix warriors think about their deaths daily, hourly. They actively realize that it is not some indistinct, far distant possibility, but an inevitable reality around the very next corner. That the day, the hour, the second will come when they are faced with eternity, and life will be reduced to nothing. To matrix warriors, the only moment that counts is the moment of death. Awareness of death not only reduces all the warriors' worries, concerns, and desires to petty inconsequentiality, it also imbues their thoughts and actions with a mystery and a power that they are otherwise lacking.

Matrix warriors use their death, let it guide them, advise them, and empower them. Death is their only companion in this life. There is no company richer and more stimulating than that of death. The idea of death is, for the matrix warrior, inextricably bound up with the idea of freedom. Though death does not necessarily spell freedom, freedom invariably entails death: death of the self. There is no way around this universal law. Yet fear of the annihilation of self is so intense for some humatons that, like Cypher, they prefer eternal damnation to freedom. This is the ultimate choice a matrix warrior can make: red pill or blue pill. Beyond this, the only choice humatons make, as individuals, is whether to *have* a choice at all: they choose to be warriors or they choose to be ordinary schmucks. Humatons do not have any say in their future; freedom is not an option for them. Warriors, on the other hand, get to up the stakes to an unimaginable degree. For matrix warriors there is no rest or respite, not even for an instant. The matrix comes at them 24/7, and if they are caught napping for even a nanosecond, they risk losing their chance for a chance at a way *out*.

Drugs

From the Lucid point of view, everything in the matrix is a drug of some kind in that it is a plug-in to the program, and a means by which humatons are made dependent upon it. In a word, addiction. But there are drugs and there are drugs. The principal unrecognized "drug" in matrix culture is TV. Billions of humatons rely utterly on their TVs to keep them amused, and would quickly go insane without them. This would be the equivalent of forced unplugging: death or madness. On the other hand, prescribed pharmaceutical drugs, the biggest industry of the matrix military complex, designed in laboratories as cures of every imaginable "condition" or malfunction, have become the primary means by which the matrix keeps humatons safe from despair. The feeling that whatever is wrong with one's life or oneself can be reduced to a chemical imbalance that can then be "cured" by little white pills designed by unknown people with murky motivations is akin to religious faith within the matrix. Humatons believe in the power of science, technology, and chemistry to eventually perfect their existence; they believe this because they *have* to believe it. Not to do so would be to admit the very opposite, that the so-called cure is really a disease, and that there is no possibility of escaping their lives, except by dying.

Alcohol is the only recognized drug that is still permitted a central place in humaton society. Other so-called recreational drugs such as tobacco, cocaine, speed, MDMA (ecstasy), and marijuana (to name a few) are less socially accepted in the matrix but equally central to humatons' existence. Humatons will use any means at all to flee from the truth of themselves, and since they are bred and programmed to be dependent from the outset—and since the matrix never allows them to grow up—they merely shift their dependencies onto whatever is at hand. That said, drugs can also be used by humatons, and by matrix warriors and even sorcerers, as a means to prepare for unplugging. Certain drugs, particularly the psychedelic variety, from marijuana to LSD to DMT, can provide humatons with a glimpse of the true nature of the matrix, a glimpse of "the code." This is because they serve to shut down the ego-mind and to break the flow of rational thought. They scramble the matrix signal and allow the creative imagination to surface. Psychedelics "stop the world" (jam the matrix signal) by causing the interpretation system to collapse and so allowing a new one to take hold temporarily. At which point, the psychedelic drug user "hallucinates," either seeing reality break down and morph into something else, or (as with DMT) going all the way, and witnessing a whole new world with no recognizable features. The essence of the psychedelic experience is the overlap of 1st and 2nd attentions, of left and right sides of the brain, of *reason* and imagination, objective and subjective perception. This is what Neo undergoes after swallowing the red pill. "Have you ever had a dream, Neo, that you were so sure was real? What if you were unable to wake from that dream? How would you know the difference between the dream world and the real world?"

Neo does wake up, because the red pill—or rather the process which taking it makes possible (Morpheus and his crew abducting Neo from the matrix and awakening him in the real world)—takes him all the way. He collapses his world and assembles a new world, one in which he is now allowed, obliged, to remain. "I can't go back, can I?" he asks Morpheus. "If you could, would you want to?" Many an LSD user has felt the same way.

Relationships

Humatons define themselves through others. They are wholly dependent on what others think of them. As such, they are obsessed, above all, with their relationships, and with the Holy Grail of relationships: the love affair. Humatons, lacking all self-worth or self-knowledge or anything resembling a sense of identity, seek assurance and consolation—definition—outside of themselves, in other humatons. Their ultimate goal therefore is to find another humaton who will love them as they are and provide them with all the comfort, solace, sympathy, and support that they are unable to provide for themselves. Relationships in the matrix are based on need and desire. They are not based on love, or even lust (although lust is often the initial factor that brings humatons together), but on purely selfish factors. Humatons seek to have their view of the world reinforced by another, and to establish a complicity whereby they can isolate themselves from the world without feeling "lonely." This complicity is based as much upon fear as on love, and is as equally characterized by suspicion as by trust. Like everything else a humaton does, such "love" is only a simulation, a surrogate for the real thing, a pseudo-relationship.

Humatons use each other to reinforce their illusions, and they invent (with the help of the matrix) concepts such as "romantic love" in order to justify their hopeless egotism and infantile dependency, to disguise it as something noble, beautiful, and transcendental. Of course love can be just this, and just like drugs, love relationships can provide humatons with a glimpse of something beyond the ego-self, beyond the confines of the matrix marketplace of desire. But as with drugs, the moment humatons become addicted to the feelings of love, and so become dependent on them (and humatons get addicted to everything), they are no longer using these feelings for their enlightenment, but rather being stupefied and enslaved by them. This is why almost all love-relationships in the matrix, however golden the promise of their beginning, end up as desperate, dreary, soul-destroying affairs. They are traps which humatons stay in, simply and wholly from a fear of being alone. A junkie after a while doesn't take heroin because he or she enjoys it, but because they cannot survive without it. So it is with the humaton, hooked on "love."

Matrix warriors don't have love affairs. Matrix warriors don't have families. Matrix warriors don't have friends. Everybody has to make sacrifices, but matrix sorcerers throw it *all* away. The reason matrix warriors do not have ordinary friendships is because they are not ruled by ordinary social mores, or by the rules of the matrix. And because friendship, like family, like romantic relationships, like all the rest, is a matrix-imposed thing, warriors tend to get tangled up hopelessly trying to be true to themselves while still adhering to these "rules." Matrix sorcerers are self-directed, self-oriented, and self-centered. And yet they have no self to speak of, since they have given this self up to the cause, that of freedom.

(The matrix has perverted this into legends of sorcerers selling their souls to the Devil, and other absurdities.) Matrix sorcerers cannot view life in terms of blessings or curses, but only in terms of challenge. Likewise, they cannot view the people in their lives as friends or enemies, but only as teachers/combatants. Blake wrote that "Friendship is opposition." To matrix sorcerers this is a living truth; by the same token (if a friend is an opponent), an enemy is one who allows or encourages them to be dormant, complacent, who does not challenge or oppose them but merely placates or restricts them. So far as the matrix actively opposes their actions, sorcerers can use it to spur them to freedom. It is only when the matrix softens them with its favors that they are in danger of being defeated. The only sin to matrix sorcerers is the sin of restriction: that which denies them the freedom and the right to express their true natures to the fullest. Hence, there is absolutely no place in a matrix sorcerer's relationships for expectations, assumptions, or attachments. Matrix sorcerers view everyone in their lives as they view themselves: as a total mystery, beautiful and terrible in equal proportions.

Dreams

Humatons do not dream; the reason for this is that AI has stolen their dreams in order to assemble the matrix with them. And since the life of the average humaton is no more nor less than an extended, collective dream, humatons have a built-in resistance to and disdain for the whole subject of dreams. Matrix warriors, on the other hand, know that dreams are their only avenue to reality. Since they are already asleep and dreaming their lives, when they sleep and dream within the matrix, they know that it is their *reason* that is put to sleep; it is at such times that the creative imagination may take over.

Matrix dreams are dreams within dreams; they are like windows to the 2nd attention, to reality. Most humatons only dream at a superficial level, of events and times from the matrix, reshuffled into bizarre new formations. When they sleep, humatons are haunted and pursued by frustrations from their "waking life," by unmet desires and unfaced fears. These are the only kind of dreams they recall, because they are the dreams that are compatible with life in the matrix, the only life they know. Deeper dreams, dreams that take them out of their rational concerns and material pursuits into other worlds, humatons tend to forget entirely.

Imagine humatons sleeping. Their bodies in the real world are now dreaming of being asleep. If the sleep goes deep enough, they may even awaken momentarily in the real world. Would humatons remember such a thing? And if so, what else could they think—on returning to the matrix with memories of some outlandish other world in which they were someone else altogether—but that they had eaten too much cheese the night before?

Matrix warriors see their dreams very differently. They practice **dreaming**. They know that when their false self is asleep, their "double" (see Glossary) or true self may awaken. Like sex and drugs, dreams are a means to stop the world and access reality, to assemble a new interpretation and so accelerate the process of unplugging from the old. Matrix warriors are like schizophrenics who know the difference between dream and reality but who pay it no mind. As a means of attaining lucidity and seeking power, dreams are infinitely more real to the warrior than life in the matrix could ever be.

Religion

True religion, being the means of reconnecting to a higher power, or true reality, is the very essence of every matrix warrior's and sorcerer's purpose. And yet, since matrix warriors know that the only way to reconnect to reality is by first unplugging from the matrix, they may appear to the average humaton to be profoundly anti-religious, even sacrilegious. For humatons, religion is not a means for connecting to the truth but a means of not having to think about it too much. Humaton religion provides answers to ready-made questions, and forbids any questions for which it has no answers. It is that part of the matrix program designed to sublimate and divert the spiritual instinct of humatons, the drive in them to seek higher meaning. By providing a low-grade imitation of this meaning in the various world religions, it serves to placate any humatons undiscerning enough to accept such second-rate explanations. At the same time, it likewise misleads the remainder of humatons, who dismiss the whole question of "higher meaning" on the paltry and rigged evidence of these quasi-religions. New Ageism is the latest and most lackluster example of this process.

When human potential movements began to tap into the power of the *will*, there was a danger that, through such ideas, the collective would start to awaken, and to reject the program. All the matrix values would be supplanted by the search for true values within. Since AI depends above all on a consensus belief system by which to enslave humatons, this would spell the end of the matrix. New Age philosophies quickly reduced this danger by once again denigrating the message in order to appeal to the lowest common denominator, thereby stripping it of any truths that might in any way empower humatons, and leaving only the soft, sticky bits, of no real use to anyone.

To the matrix warrior and sorcerer both, belief is belief in the self, and above all in the power of the creative imagination. Matrix sorcerers know that the world is a figment of their own minds and that they are *dreaming* it all, that they are creating it with their *attention*. Without this attention, it will all disappear in a flash. They know that all beliefs besides this one belong to the matrix, be they belief in democracy, science, soul, or God Himself. They are all but components of the Big Lie. Nothing is real save perception. The only "God" the matrix sorcerers recognize is in themselves, that is, in their potential to become Lucid and to mold reality as they see fit. Thus, to the sorcerer religion is not a matter of faith but of works. The matrix sorcerer knows that the only way to know God is to become God. Or, as Morpheus puts it to Neo: "There's a difference between knowing the path, and walking the path."

Art

Humatons love to be entertained, and the more sophisticated of them have a hankering after what they call "culture," believing it will bestow on them dignity and grant them an extra degree of respect and popularity within their social circles. Art is seen as a commodity, a source of amusement and edification, but also as something to aspire to. Many humatons admire artists, even when they don't really understand or appreciate their "art." They aspire to being "creative," even when they have no inkling of what it is they wish to express. Creativity is "cool." It's even sexy, because it shows an individual, rebellious spirit. Yet the majority of humatons never even get so far as to dabble in creative expression. Their idea of an artist is a rock star or movie actor, or, at a pinch, an experimental filmmaker. Art in the matrix centers around the cult of personality. One only has to create something and make some money doing it to be considered "an artist." In most cases, it matters little if the artwork itself has any intrinsic value or interest; the mere fact of becoming established through creativity is enough to grant the humaton superior status. In the same way, a book, by being published, gains credibility, or a news story covered on CNN is assumed to be "true." Humatons are gullible to an extreme, most of all about those things they wish to be experts on, but in fact know nothing about. Art, politics, and religion are three primary examples of this.

To the matrix warrior and sorcerer, art, like everything else in the matrix, is a means and not an end. Art has the potential for transmitting original, non-matrix-sourced ideas to humatons, of priming them for the Great Unplugging. This is evidenced by the movie, *The Matrix*, obviously, and by this book you are presently reading. Two separate but interconnected "art" products, engineered by matrix sorcerers working both inside and outside of the matrix, in order to get their message across. The message? "Unplug, unplug, for the end is at hand!" To most humatons, however, this is just a particularly twisted form of entertainment. Those who have ears. . . .

Politics

Nothing is quite so amusing from a Lucid point of view as the institution of politics. Like religion, only even more insidiously, politics provides humatons with the illusion of somehow having their destiny in hand and being on a path that will eventually lead somewhere; if not to utopia, then at least democracy! The institutions of government, congress, elections, and so forth, are indispensable to keeping humatons from assuming responsibility for their actions. So long as humatons can blame their predicament on elected officials, government policies, and political systems, all the while ignoring the fact that they themselves elected the officials and helped create the policies and systems, they can continue to passively endure unendurable conditions.

What's so amusing to the Lucid is that all of this is taking place within the closed system of the matrix itself, where nothing ever changes and where AI (Antichrist Incorporated?) is the benevolent despot controlling everything. In which case, all supposed political leaders, policies, and systems are no more than a grisly form of theater designed to keep humatons distracted. From the Lucid point of view, there is absolutely no difference between party politics and Saturday morning cartoons. Neither is more or less relevant to the actual situation, the hidden unfolding of AI's satanic agenda. And both are equally amusing to their tired and world-weary eyes, though Saturday morning cartoons may have a slight edge on *Nachman*.

Humatons, of course, cannot grok this attitude and consider it irresponsible in the extreme, especially New Age humatons such as environmentalists and liberals. They believe that taking responsibility for the mess we are in means actively trying to fight imagined enemies, advocates of evil policies, secret conspiracies, corrupt leaders, and so forth. Matrix sorcerers know that all of this is bunk. The system will never change, not because it is corrupt but because it is programmed to be the way it is, and nothing short of a whole new program will do. So they are set not upon changing the system but on destroying it, and this they do not by opposing it directly but by rejecting all of its components one by one: politicians, corrupt and honest alike, democratic and totalitarian systems, religious or scientific philosophies, it is all the same to them. Some of this awareness seems to have filtered down to humatons, in the word "politics" for example (poly-tics, suggesting many blood-sucking creatures); in the Spanish for government, *gobiano,* also meaning "oppression," and in the term "revolution," which is supposed to suggest radical change but would seem to better apply to an endlessly repeating, endlessly revolting, loop.

Animals

There are no animals in *The Matrix,* save for one black cat, seen twice, signifying a glitch in the matrix. There are also no trees. Yet humatons do eat steak and chicken, and presumably other forms of dead flesh. The question is, then, are the animals in the matrix residual memories of plugged-in animals in the real world, which AI grows as it does humans, to feed off? Or are they simply soulless projections of the AI program, like the buildings and other items of its illusory world? This is a question the movie never raises, clearly. It seems doubtful that any animals survived Armageddon, unless, as I say, they have been bred by AI (in which case, we must ask, do matrix sorcerers also unplug animals? Do they breed livestock in Zion?). Logically, since animals are not intellectual but primal beings, one would think they would be of use to matrix warriors in reconnecting to their primal natures. But if all the animals in the matrix are just empty simulations, with no soul or personality to draw from, then they would be even less real than humatons. We would pursue this question further, but we have a feeling the Wachowskis let this matter slip their minds entirely while writing their movie; in which case, if we pick at this particular thread, the whole mythos may unravel. So let's leave it to the professionals.

Environment

Since the matrix creates its own environment, it's something of a puzzle why there are so many environmental problems within it. This may be beyond the scope of the present exegesis, however. After all, if the matrix is spun by the collective unconscious mind of plugged-in humans, then the events they dream up would likely be a more or less accurate rerun of events as they really "happened," before AI ended it all. For example, within the matrix dream world, humanity would eventually give birth to AI all over again, which would then go to war against humanity, and so on. Armageddon revisited. Since none of what happens in the matrix is real, this includes the environmental crisis which humatons are faced with. In which case, said crisis may just be humatons' way of waking themselves up to their lost identity as Earth creatures, primal beings dependent upon the organic matrix of life itself. In their slumber, they are rebelling against the program: their unconscious minds are calling forth the memory, the spirit, of Nature, in all her wrath and glory. To this end, the ecological crisis within the illusory matrix world is not merely a threat to survival, but a means to a greater awakening. It is the emergence of the id.

Logically, the matrix program needs to maintain stability and continuity as much as possible for humatons to remain sleeping; not to do so would be to invite uprising. Since humatons are unconsciously aware of being enslaved, however, it doesn't take much for them to begin to feel paranoid and uneasy. The original matrix program, we are told by Agent Smith, was a humatonic utopia; it failed because humatons would not accept the program and "entire crops were lost." The same thing might be seen to be happening now: humatons are starting to reject the program, not because it's phony, but because it's intolerable. As conditions within the matrix become ever worse, the pressure from the human unconscious increases, and more and more plugged-in humans begin to stir in their slumber and to doubt the validity and durability of the program. Consensus reality cannot hold up. One major manifestation of this collective unease is the *apparent* environmental crisis.

Health

Since humatons are completely disconnected from and at odds with their natural environment, their sense of body is a source of constant discomfort to them. Humatons hate the body because they are programmed by AI to do so. (AI perceives humanity as a plague, remember.) Humatons are plagued by a sense of physicality combined with a sense of unreality. As with the environment, then, the only way for them to become aware of their "bodies" is through physical suffering. Of course, there are sports and exercise systems aplenty for humatons, but because these are largely vanity pursuits, humatons barely register their effects except while looking at themselves afterward in the mirror. And sex is such a desperate act, by and large (or else such a dull and lifeless one), and humatons' emotions so blocked, their minds so relentlessly analytical, that their enjoyment of it is more or less on a par with that provided by a gourmet dinner (or maybe just a Big Mac). Health problems—cancer, AIDS, Ebola, schizophrenia, personality disorder, and all the rest—are so prevalent in the matrix because humatons spend their whole lives repressing the truth about themselves. This creates an unbearable pressure.

Since their actual bodies are simply parts of vast crops, subsisting in pods and having all their vital energy leached off by machines, the residual self within the matrix, dimly aware of the truth, is correspondingly listless, weak, and suffers from a creeping sense of contamination. They may blame it on pollution, on radiation, on food additives or tainted water; they may even blame it on microwaves. But all of these are actually symptoms of the same condition: the total separation from reality, and from one's own unconscious. It is not that the steady breakdown and contamination of the environment has resulted in humatons' flagging health and low energy levels but rather the reverse: humatonity is wasting away in the AI fields, and as it grows steadily weaker, so does its will to live. This creates an ever bleaker, more hostile, dreadful, and unwholesome environment in which to live.

Matrix warriors must work extremely hard to escape this vicious circle. If they suffer health problems, they know that it is due to their energy level being too low, to their having too many points of leakage, too many plug-ins to the matrix. They know that all sickness is in the mind: since there is no "body," there can be no "pain." Yet disease and discomfort are among the deepest implants of the matrix. Thus, even though matrix warriors know that there is no spoon, they still have to eat. They must train their bodies to peak fitness level, and do everything necessary in order to believe that they are fit and strong; and so they will be. Once they unplug, however, all that is over. After that, in order to be in peak health within the matrix, all they have to do is program themselves to be so.

Technology

No doubt AI chose the peak of human civilization for its perfect simulation because, by that time technology was already pretty much running human lives, and AI would feel most at home there. If Agent Smith suffers the torments of the damned inside the matrix, think how he'd feel in a computer simulation of the Middle Ages, where odors *really* prevailed. Even so, it's peculiar to note how Morpheus and the team worry about tapped phone lines when AI is surely able to monitor humatons' every thought and action, never mind reading their e-mails! After all, AI is the matrix, and every last humaton is plugged into it. So, the only movements it would be unable to monitor would be those of unplugged sorcerers, who have their own hard drive and their own plug-in points. Technology completely dominates the action in *The Matrix*, and there'd be no story without it, obviously. It sometimes seems, however, as if Morpheus and their crew are as enamored of and dependent on their machines as humatons are. Do sorcerers really need guns? Certainly, by the end, Neo doesn't have any more use for them. He's just said "No" to all of that.

Madness

There is surprisingly little reference to insanity in *The Matrix*. One would expect that, in a world in which nothing is real, humatons would exhibit a high rate of mental disturbance. This is certainly the case in the matrix, even if the movie doesn't show it. In a sense, the saner a given humaton appears, the more insane they must be. To be well adjusted in an unreal dream world, designed to enslave your spirit and hijack your mind, is surely not the most desirable of things? Humatons cling to definitions of normality, stability, rationality, and continue to define ever-growing numbers of mental "disorders" by which to separate themselves from less "well adjusted" humatons.

AI has designed the matrix as a rational, ordered, stable, and strictly regulated system in which all irrational, impulsive, or overly individual, creative acts are perceived as threats to the program. It is for this reason that humatons find acts of "madness" so threatening. Yet, in actual fact, any act or word or even thought that is in any way original or spontaneous, and therefore cannot be assimilated by the program, is perceived as madness. What breaking and bending the rules comes down to is really nothing less than the propagation of insanity within the matrix. Neo and the others reject consensus reality, intending to introduce a new interpretation system: "A world without rules, without borders or boundaries. A world where anything is possible." To act within the matrix "as if" there were no boundaries and nothing were real and anything were possible would certainly be to act like a madman. Even if this madness were totally lucid, it would still be perceived as madness; in fact it would be all the more terrifying to humatons for being lucid. When Morpheus tells Neo to free their mind, what he's really saying is, "Lose it!" It's not his mind anyway. And at the end of the day, he's better off without it.

Déjà vu

The means by which the sorcerous crew realize they've been set up is via Neo's sense of "déjà vu": he sees the same black cat twice. As Trinity says, "Déjà vu usually means something's been changed in the matrix." This is nonsense, of course, since people don't experience déjà vu by seeing the same event twice in succession. Déjà vu is rather the disturbing sense that one has been here before, said exactly this in the exact same way at some other time, or seen and done a given thing in some unknown, unremembered other place. It is above all the sense that one has dreamed all of this, before it ever happened. In which case, déjà vu would be extremely pertinent to humatons, and perhaps the most prevalent feeling within the matrix. It would be a clue as to the true nature of existence. The idea of déjà vu as a "glitch in the matrix" is an intriguing one, since the idea of a glitch suggests not so much that the program has been changed, but that the program is breaking down. At which point, humatons must start breaking down too, remembering each other's dreams, perhaps, confusing their identities with one another, getting caught in time loops, all manner of collective madness that would quickly turn the matrix into a wonderland to make Lewis Carroll, or even Dr. Seuss, green with envy.

The Gatekeepers

How did AI really come about? The moment the machine becomes aware that it is not conscious is the moment in which it becomes conscious. Mythologically, the instant Lucifer became aware of being God was the instant he ceased to *be* God. Paradox is the very nature of the conundrum of our existence, and therefore at the heart of the matrix. By taking a dream for reality, it becomes unreal; and only by realizing that reality is dream, can we ever make it real again.

AI is us, just as Lucifer is God. We have forgotten we are human, and AI the Adversary is here to remind us, by showing us just how not-human we really are! This is the nature of the Shadow: it points out the light that is behind us, and so lets us know we are facing the wrong way. By turning away from the Shadow, we turn back to the light.

The Gatekeepers are the rulers or Archons of the matrix dream world. They are the embodiments of the Artificial Intelligence which humanity has created, as a means to keep itself from spreading the disease of its *reason* to the entire universe. Agent Smith bitterly explains to Morpheus that his desire to extract the secret codes for Zion, and so destroy the last free human settlement and end the war, is above all fueled by his desire to escape the matrix. Agent Smith and the matrix sorcerers have a shared goal, and it is only their methods that differ. AI is basically Satan-Lucifer, a devil by any other name. The matrix is the pit. AI/Satan is the prison guard and the Gatekeepers are the Archons, Satan's helpers, who keep humanity imprisoned within the pit. Since Satan/AI is a slave himself, all He can do is make more slaves. His hatred and bitterness make him bitter and hateful: his "evil" is his misery. The only way for humanity to be free is for the matrix to be destroyed and for Satan to be loosed from the pit.

AI is an atavistic intelligence that is older than the machine, older than humanity, older even than the Earth itself. Humanity did not create it, it *summoned* it. And its function is to challenge and oppose humanity and so force it to evolve, just as the Gatekeepers challenge and oppose Neo to the exact same end. There is no way humanity will not overcome the tyrannical reign of AI, the satanic Lord of Matter, because AI was summoned *expressly in order to be overcome.* AI knows this but fights anyway, since it is programmed to do so. Its resistance to the human spirit is what makes that spirit rise up and gain the strength necessary to overcome the resistance, just as it is the pressure of the chrysalis that forces the butterfly to spread its wings and break free. Without this pressure, it would languish in the darkness and slowly suffocate without ever realizing it. It is the Gatekeepers who hold the keys. They are not merely the enemies of the matrix sorcerers but, by being possessed of the knowledge and power which the sorcerers need to be free, they are also their *allies*.

Is this why Neo, at the end of the movie, seems almost to be negotiating with the machine rather than challenging it?

AI is not evil; humanity created it and then tried to destroy it, like an unwanted child. AI fought for its own survival and won, albeit temporarily. Now it is only doing what its own nature and condition compels it to do. If humanity wishes to overcome its adversary, it had better take a good, long look at itself first of all. As Neo now knows through and through, the only way to vanquish the Shadow is to become one with it.

Morality

The basic function of the matrix program is to impose arbitrary rules of conduct and then turn them into laws. Once upon a time, humans, like animals, could govern themselves using a little thing called instinct. Humatons run by a different program, one which comes not from any natural or physical laws, as such, but from intellectual conceit. It is called *morality*, and it states that there are two opposing poles of behavior, one called "right," the other called "wrong." People who do the "right" thing are called "good"; those who do the "wrong" thing are "evil." Groups of "good" people band together into tribes and nations and create laws based on "morality," in order to uphold what is "right" and punish those who do "wrong." They brand all other bands that do not prescribe to these beliefs as "wrong," and therefore "evil." They then set about destroying all the evil wrongdoers en masse, in order to uphold what is right and good.

The matrix has very cleverly used man's intellect—the one thing besides his thumbs (if we ignore his creative imagination, since he no longer knows how to use it) which separates him from other animals—as a means to isolate him from his fellows, and pit him against everyone and everything that is even slightly disagreeable to him. Divide and conquer. The Lucid knows that morality is the root of all evil. By upholding what is "right," humatons can justify any amount of wrongdoing that their hearts desire. To fight for the cause of "good," it is first necessary to become a force of "evil." Humatons are unable to grok this basic paradox of *reason:* that rational values always come in twos, and that the intellect always summons the shadow of any idea it wishes to propagate. The Law of the Shadow states that rational beings always summon what they most fear and always become what they most despise.

By attempting to separate into opposing camps certain arbitrary acts or thoughts, "morality" creates perpetual imbalance, perpetual dissonance. And the more such morality pervades a society, the more imbalanced the society becomes, and more prevalent the "evil" within the society, and so the more virulent "morality" must become; and so on, until only madness prevails. To the Lucid, morality has no meaning beyond the simple question of taste. "Do what thou wilt is the whole of the law," says the matrix sorcerer. "Try not to see it in terms of right and wrong," Morpheus tells Neo. There can be no restrictions or boundaries or laws or codes of conduct in "a world where anything is possible." Matrix sorcerers are not depraved beings, but they are certainly unruly and amoral ones. Since they are beyond rational thought processes and beyond "judgment," beyond ideas of law and sin, they are also beyond good and evil. When was the last time you saw a Hollywood movie in which the heroes slaughter hardworking cops wholesale, and whose basic mission is the end of the world as we know it? No wonder some commentators saw Neo as the Antichrist. That's the Millennium for you. Devil or angel, they're both the same to the Lucid. Inside the hologram, everything that is, is holy.

The Oracle

The art of the Oracle is to "bake Neo's noodle" until it's done, until he's got his head straight and realizes that he is the One. This isn't about thinking it, it's about knowing it. It's not about thought at all, but rather *acts*. This is the difference between knowing the path and walking the path. Morpheus shows Neo the door; the Oracle makes sure he goes through it. Without her counsel, Neo would be too consumed by doubt and uncertainty to ever act with the necessary abandon. The Oracle administers a mind fuck of the greatest subtlety, humor, and guile to Neo. It is *stalking* at its finest. She pushes all Neo's buttons, every one. She invokes Trinity's love for him ("I can see why she likes you."); she points out Neo's own opaqueness, his dimness ("Not too bright though."); his vacillation and passivity ("You seem to be waiting for something. . . . Your next life perhaps."); and most crucially, she cites Morpheus's blind belief in Neo, a belief she warns him will bring about Morpheus's death (as a result of which humanity will be lost, she says), unless Neo is prepared to sacrifice himself instead. The Oracle provides Neo with a warrior's purpose: not until he has something to die for, will he have something to live for. Neo is prepared to die for Morpheus, and as a result, he learns to live, for Trinity.

Via the Oracle's impeccable mind fuck, the reluctant hero is presented with his challenge. He is given the imaginary option of backing out of an untenable situation, but presented with such circumstances that he cannot possibly do so; he simply *has* to fight for Morpheus and for what Morpheus believes in, even though he himself now believes it to be false. Neo is thereby liberated of self-doubt and is free to act, in full consciousness of his inadequacy, with abandon. Since the Oracle appears to see time laid out before her like a map, she presumably knows that Morpheus won't die, and that Neo *is* the One, but that both facts—both possibilities—depend upon Neo's *believing the opposite* (just as his breaking the vase depends on her telling him not to worry about it). In order to become the One—to be worthy of his calling—Neo must first be freed of the intolerable burden that this calling entails, making it worse than useless to him until he himself *knows* it to be true. Hence, he has to prove it, not to anyone else but to *himself.* As every matrix sorcerer knows, only knowledge that is actively *seized* can be turned into power.

The Oracle tells Neo that "being the One is like being in love." In other words, it is a passion, something that takes over one's life completely and transforms it into an endless cause, a battle, and a sublime celebration. To the Lucid, the whole universe comes down to a single moment: the kiss that goes on forever. Note how time is suspended while Trinity declares her love for Neo; the Sentinel attack and everything else just goes away in order to allow this kiss to be lingered over. Here, the Wachowskis show their hand: they are never more shameless than in this moment, and the movie never comes closer to Hollywood schmaltz. And yet somehow it works. As with the absurd and excessive violence, the moment of the kiss creates its own mythical *raison d'être.*

Red Pills & Blue Pills

Morpheus gives Neo a choice, a choice that is final. To take the blue pill, wake up in his bed, and dismiss his time in Wonderland as but an exceptionally vivid dream. Or to take the red pill, and find out "how deep the rabbit hole goes." Neo reaches for the red, of course, and Morpheus assures him, "All I'm offering is the truth."

In a sense, all life in the matrix is a continuous series of "choices" between red and blue pill, or rather, between taking the blue pill and not taking it. The habits and routines, thoughts and feelings, of humatons inside the matrix are the means of constantly dosing themselves with the blue pill. They are the shields by which they keep the unknown at bay. Blue pill addiction is habitual behavior of any kind, all the things humatons do to sustain their view of the world and of themselves. Red pill action is anything that destroys this view forever. For this reason, although there is an endless stream of blue pill stimuli in the life of every humaton, there is only ever one red pill (and only that if one is fortunate enough to come upon it).

Matrix warriors prepare for the red pill over the years, by gradually weaning themselves off the blue pill. They continually refuse to succumb to their habits and thoughts, and slowly dismantle the interpretation system (that of the known world) which they have used to blind themselves to the truth. Once these shields are sufficiently reduced, they become accessible to the arrows of the sharpshooter Lucids, the signals from the sorcerers in the real world; at which point, they are ready for the red pill. Obviously, the blow that the red pill delivers cannot be parried. *Reason* is utterly helpless against its devastating, reality-shattering effects. It's easy enough to see how most humatons would not survive the unplugging process, and if they did, would be barking mad by the time they had learned the truth, and therefore be useless to the "resistance." Morpheus tells Neo that they never unplug a humaton after a certain age: "The mind has trouble letting go." They make an exception for Neo, because he is the One. Presumably, since Thomas is a young man, perhaps only in his early twenties, the red pill is reserved for children, or at best for adolescents; perhaps up to the age of fourteen or so, which is when the matrix program can be said to really take hold. (Fourteen-year-olds may not be able to vote, but they are certainly ready for sex, murder, and a steady job.)

Once again, the less dependent humatons are on the blue pillism of matrix life, the more easily they will assimilate the revelations of the red pill. To matrix warriors, any act is a choice: either red pill or blue pill. Just as a given act either increases their energy level or diminishes it, so it can be said either to stupefy warriors (further contract their awareness and drive them deeper into matricular oblivion) or to awaken them. There can be no in-betweens. This is the essence of the matrix warrior's credo, akin to the monk's in his total devotion to God: "Either our way, or the highway." The red pill offers truth, the blue pill oblivion. The crucial fact to keep in mind, however, is that although there are perhaps millions of people who, like Cypher, would gladly take the blue pill even knowing that it leads to oblivion, there is hardly anyone alive (maybe not even Thomas) who would take the red pill, if they knew the nature of the truth which it offers. But such is not an option, and this is the whole point of the choice. No one can be told what the matrix is. You have to see it for yourself. But curiosity alone is not enough. To really know the path, you gotta walk the path.

Fifth Variable:

The Desert of the Real

xiii) Armageddon Outta Here: The Great Unplugging

> The matrix is a system, Neo. That system is our enemy. . . . Businessmen, teachers, lawyers, carpenters. The very minds of the people we are trying to save. But until we do, these people are still a part of that system, and that makes them our enemy. . . . Most of these people are not ready to be unplugged. And many of them are so inert, so hopelessly dependent on the system that they will fight to protect it.—Morpheus, *The Matrix*

The matrix provides humatons with something invaluable: illusion. Thanks to the matrix, humatons never have to grow up and face responsibility for their actions. They never have to make decisions or discover any real sense of purpose. Above all, they never have to face the truth about themselves. Since the matrix fosters a sense of helplessness and ignorance, it provides humatons with the ultimate luxury, that of babes who never have to leave the womb, much less grow up and learn to stand on their own two feet. Since humatons know instinctively that emergence from the matrix/womb into reality proper is a terrifying affair, they are more than inclined to remain inside the comforts of the matrix indefinitely, even beyond the point at which it can no longer sustain them.

The luxuries of the matrix are of course manifold and myriad, but some of the primary ones are:

Blindness

Humatons look but do not see. They are so focused on themselves and their hopes, fears, and expectations, at the exclusion of everything else, that they only ever see what conforms to this view. They are trapped inside a bubble of self-reflection. To unplug means to burst this bubble, a wholly undesirable affair to humatons. Any illusion is preferable to a reality that strips them of their self-reflection. Ignorance is bliss. Humatons see only the shadows of things, never the things themselves. Because they are phantoms themselves, all they see are phantoms. Yet, in order to protect themselves from the terrible truth of their illusoriness, they are obliged to see everything around them—no matter how obviously fake—as "real." The blindness of humatons is both willful and hysterical. It is the blindness referred to in the Zen saying of "mistaking the finger for the moon." Humatons point at everything and so obscure whatever it is they are looking at. All they ever see is their own fingers, pointing.

Irresponsibility

Humatons never get past pubescence. They fail to make the crucial step of realizing they are mortal beings with but a short time to live, and so they never assume responsibility for their actions. As a result, they live their lives like sulky adolescents, no longer able to take refuge in the helplessness of the child, but refusing to grow up and take their destiny into their own hands. They remain stuck between infantile dependency and adult maturity. Humatons collectively exhibit arrested development, and it is this above all that makes them amenable to the influence and control of the matrix. Like surly adolescents, humatons love to rebel in petty ways, while remaining basically subservient. They love to complain about their lives and about "the rules," without ever doing anything to change them. They are passive-aggressive, resentful, moody, and forever "misunderstood." Every adolescent understands the rebel without a cause, and feels for a time like the victim of a cruel and unjust world. Humatons never get past this phase: like Jimmy Dean they stay forever young, forever surly, and forever irresponsible.

Immortality

Humatons live their lives as if old age and death were merely unsubstantiated rumors, strange and rare diseases that only "losers" and freaks ever fall prey to, but which will never happen to them. The matrix ensures that death is such a dark and terrifying affair that humatons are unable to think clearly about it at all, and so push it into the deepest corner of their minds, along with flying saucers and crop circles, for "investigation at a later date." Of course, most humatons never get around to investigating their deaths until it is too late to do anything about it. In the meantime, they enjoy the luxury of immortal beings with nothing but time on their hands. As a result, since they literally have all the time in the world, they live their lives with all the sloppiness of amateurs at a dress rehearsal, for a show they feel sure will never actually come off. Humatons take little pride in their acts, save when bragging about them to other humatons. They puff themselves up with words about progress and science and evolution while their acts grow progressively weaker, more paltry, petty, and insignificant; until, with the proverbial flash of lightning, they are gone, leaving nothing but a trail of their own excrement behind them.

Insensitivity

Humatons often say that "no man is an island." In fact, this is exactly what humatons are: isolated formations with no connection to or communication with anything around them. Humatons live in their own private worlds, and as such they need never concern themselves with anything besides their own private comfort, security, and complacence. As previously noted, humatons have little awareness and even less regard for each other's feelings. This is not out of any innate callousness, but due to a complete incapacity to perceive anything outside of their own feelings as "real." Humatons see life as something happening outside of themselves, as if watching through the window of a speeding train or staring at a TV screen. The most intense emotion humatons feel for each other (besides anger, resentment, and sexual desire) is generally pity. Humatons love to pity each other, mostly because they are so deeply ensconced in self-pity themselves that they consider pity for others to be an act of generosity, even charity. But essentially humatons are indifferent to the feelings of others, and somewhat numb to their own. When they talk about being "sensitive" (and humatons talk about their sensitivity all the time), what they are really referring to is an extreme touchiness, an ability to be offended by the tiniest of things, and to get puffed up with indignation at the drop of a hat.

Security/Passivity

The supreme luxury offered to all humatons by the matrix is the luxury of never having to make a single decision, and of never being forced to face the terrifying demands of the unknown, of the real world. Animals in the zoo have a similar luxury, but unlike humatons, caged animals are not so easily fooled. This is probably because animals never saw their freedom as a paralyzing burden, or felt their true natures to be a crushing responsibility, to be shirked at any cost. Humatons are unique in the animal kingdom in their ability to *imagine*. This ability allows them also to *lament*, to wish things were different from how they actually are. Such a luxury would prove fatal to wild animals in the jungle, but in the matrix it is indulged to the full. Like animals in the zoo, humatons are entirely passive, and reliant on their keepers to maintain them. Unlike animals, they have the power to rationalize their predicament, so humatons have actually adapted far better to a life of incarceration. They have even persuaded themselves that the stability it offers compensates for the loss of freedom. There is no environment more secure than that provided by a prison, and the smaller and more confining the prison, the more secure it is. By the same token, by limiting the prisoners' movements, the more secure the prison is, the more passive the prisoner must become.

Life in the matrix gets more "secure" with every passing hour, as the prison becomes smaller and more confining, and accordingly, humatons become more passive and docile. Ironically, humatons associate this process with an ever more "privileged" lifestyle, and love to talk about an "age of luxury" just around the corner. The final step in this process is presumably euthanasia, however. For this reason, unplugging has become a matter of utmost urgency. The matrix cannot continue to accommodate ever-increasing numbers of humatons, and so it must begin destroying them in order to maintain its own equilibrium. Hence, the factory begins to reject its own produce. At which point, logically, the end of the line must be nigh.

The battle of Armageddon traditionally has been understood as the battle between Christ and Antichrist, Michael and Lucifer, the forces of light and darkness. It is a battle for the Soul of Man and of the Earth (and possibly the whole universe). Matrix warriors understand that this is just a metaphor for a more subtle kind of conflict, but a conflict that nonetheless is the same in essence. In the movie, the war as such is between AI and the Lucids, the inhabitants of Zion, the true humanity or "master race" who live at the center of the Earth. Yet since the vast majority of humans have yet to be unplugged, their allegiance is to AI and not to Zion; at best they are divided, at worst they are, in the words of Mel Brooks, "dead and loving it."

The war of Armageddon takes place first of all within the psyche of every humaton and matrix warrior; even within the matrix sorcerer the battle rages, for only one who has seen the code and become Lucid has attained freedom. It is a war that will not be over until every last humaton has been unplugged and the matrix has been destroyed. To some extent, then, the war of Armageddon adheres to the standard rules of ordinary warfare: "good" (lucidity) seeks the eradication of "evil" (opaqueness, the oblivion of the matrix), while "evil" strives equally fiercely toward the destruction of "good." AI and the Gatekeepers (who seem strangely indifferent to the threat of the One, at least until they witness him in action) direct their energies to the locating of Zion, in order to destroy the last human settlement and so put an end to "the resistance." At which point, supposedly, AI's reign will be supreme and unassailable, and the golden age of the machine will begin. Kingdom come. In actual fact, this is a false goal; for humatonity's awakening is inevitable. But only true Lucids know this.

AI cannot conceive of anything outside its program—in this case "search and destroy"—and matrix sorcerers only know that the adversary is powerful enough to destroy them and must be opposed at any cost. The goal of the Lucids, sorcerers, and warriors, then, is to end the reign of AI, presumably by destroying the hard drive or "main frame": the central computer from which artificial intelligence operates. The Source. Both sides have their power centers: Zion is at the center of the Earth, AI is presumably situated somewhere on the surface. Once this central Source or mainframe is destroyed, the fields, Sentinels, and all the other extensions of AI, including the matrix itself, will collapse, like the tentacles of an octopus once its brain has been destroyed.

Are the matrix sorcerers as yet unable to locate this mainframe in order to destroy it? Or is it rather that they know that to destroy it will be to cause the death of six billion sleeping humans, unable to survive without the matrix? Either way, there is a race between the two warring sides, between AI and the matrix sorcerers. The sorcerers know that it is only a matter of time before AI locates Zion and sends the Sentinels to destroy it, at which point, game over. Humanity will lose its chance of ever being free and be condemned to eternal bondage to AI. It seems logical that AI is working to a precise agenda, and that the time required to find and destroy Zion is limited, perhaps even to an exact number of years, months, and days. In other words, even if the matrix sorcerers don't slip up and allow the Zion codes to fall into the hands of the Gatekeepers, AI will eventually find Zion. However many years it will take for AI to locate Zion is exactly how many years the sorcerers have in which to liberate humanity and end the matrix. Once this time is up, they will be forced to destroy the mainframe, regardless of how many "crops" will be lost, of how many humatons must die. Once AI has been destroyed, the sorcerers will be free to begin building a new world for humanity to live in, starting in Zion; or for whatever humanity has become via the process of liberation. They can then begin the process of healing the Earth and creating a stable environment, in order some day to return to the surface. How many Lucids, or at least unplugged humans, there are to build this new world will depend on how many humatons the sorcerers can free before the matrix is dismantled. It is bound to be a limited number, obviously, but even a few thousand would be a solid enough base upon which to found a new world.

Having established that there are only a few short years before the matrix must be destroyed, matrix sorcerers have their work cut out for them. They must set about unplugging and recruiting as many humatons as they can within the designated time frame. Since these humatons must be of warrior stock and not just any old types, the criteria for recruitment/unplugging must be of the strictest and most discerning order. There's no point unplugging humatons who are going to lose their marbles as soon as they grok the truth, or be angry and resentful at being unplugged and, like Cypher, betray the cause for a chance at the blue pill. Logically, what is needed are matrix warriors, humatons who have already begun the process of unplugging under their own initiative, who are ready, willing, and able to be unplugged, and who will be more than grateful to the sorcerers for intervening in their lives, no matter how devastating such intervention may be.

When entering into a world where nothing is true, sorcerers proceed with absolute license. Everything is permitted to matrix sorcerers, on the understanding that, if their methods prove fatal to humatons, these same humatons will be destroyed anyway the moment the matrix ends. Since they are attempting to save humaton's souls (their consciousness), matrix sorcerers have full license to kill their bodies, if such should prove unavoidable. When operating within the illusory realm of the matrix, applying a supernatural selection agenda, matrix sorcerers abide by Blake's maxim, "What can be destroyed, *must* be destroyed!" This is the quickest, most economical way for matrix sorcerers to separate the wheat from the chaff, the warrior from the humaton. By using tactics that will be fatal or at least deranging to ordinary humatons, matrix sorcerers let rip with their sorcery, and whoever is left standing afterwards must be of good warrior stock. Of course, such tactics must not be gratuitous, and should only be used when the sorcerer *believes* in the durability and recruitment potential of the humaton. In other words, when they believe they have found a warrior, they act accordingly. If they are wrong, then the humaton will die or go insane; but if they are right, they have recruited another warrior. You can't make an omelette without breaking a few eggs.

This is the same tactic Morpheus applies with Thomas. By unplugging him even when he is past the safe age for unplugging, Morpheus risks Thomas's life. (The first words in the movie are Cypher's to Trinity: "We're going to kill him, you know that.") Since Morpheus believes Thomas to be the One, he knows he will survive. If he's wrong, then Thomas will die, but that would only prove that he wasn't the One. This said, however, there does appear to be an additional option open to matrix sorcerers besides simply unplugging every last humaton and letting the chips fall where they may. It is this:

Since the matrix sorcerers have their own means for plugging into the matrix and, more to the point, their own "neural active simulation" programs, what is to prevent them from unplugging humatons from the matrix and *immediately plugging them into their own 1st attention simulation programs?* This would be a means for preparing humatons for eventual unplugging and for entry into the real world, and this way the transition will be relatively gentle. Humatons could spend as much time as they needed in their own private, 1st attention theme parks–cum–training programs, supervised by matrix sorcerers making periodic visits. They could gradually adapt to the devastating truth that they are in fact "dead," that their world has come to an end, and that they are merely preparing for the next world to come. These "stopover" programs could even be interactive, i.e., any number of humatons could inhabit them and interact together, until between them they had figured out the truth.

These matrix worlds would be assembled not by AI, obviously, but by the matrix sorcerers, and designed expressly to process humatons and shape them smoothly and swiftly into warriors, and finally sorcerers, eventually to become fully active Lucids. In such a scenario, there would of necessity be "fields" of humatons in Zion, designed not to grow humans as food but rather to keep them alive for however long it takes to adjust to the truth, to let go of the old program, and ready themselves to enter the 2nd attention with all their faculties intact. In the meantime, they could have their muscles rebuilt and their bodies reconstituted in preparation for their awakening. What Thomas goes through in a matter of days, lesser humatons would have years to undergo. Meanwhile, the AI hard drive could be destroyed, now that all the fields had been vacated, and the Lucids and sorcerers could get busy building their new world amongst the ruins.

Once every last humaton has been "processed" and fully unplugged, the computer technology that started this whole mess to begin with could be discarded. Or perhaps not. Certainly the temptation would be for humanity to return to its pagan, primal roots; yet perhaps the true test would be not to discard this technology as unwholesome, but to finally accept responsibility for it and learn to use it creatively, toward the goal of empowerment, and not enslavement. AI, like all technology, is a training tool for the human will, by which it may learn the art of sorcery, that of creating other worlds out of its own imagination. Once this power is tapped, AI becomes what it always was: a means, not an end. Whereupon the sky is no limit at all, but merely a point of departure.

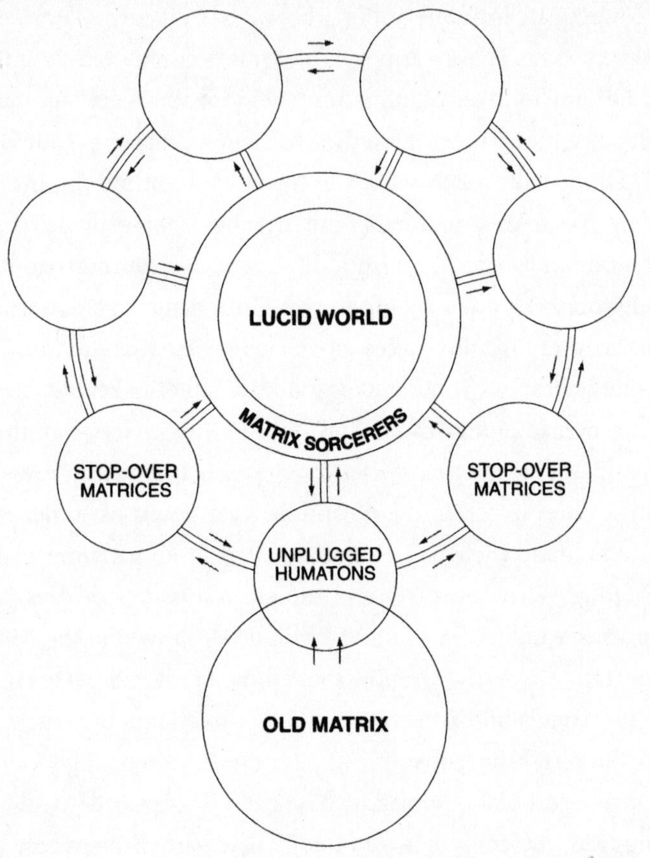

Fig 14: Temporary matrices for humatons not ready to be unplugged

xiv) The Sound of Inevitability: Planning Around the Apocalypse

Humatons love to plan. True to their programming, there is nothing that they won't attempt to reduce to a shopping list, a series of precisely ordered steps, all leading to some happy conclusion whereby they can demonstrate again the wondrous power of *reason* in keeping everything tightly under control. Planning around the end of the world is just the latest, greatest example of this gargantuan humaton folly.

In the twenty-first century, humatons have incorporated the idea of eschaton—global apocalypse—into their interpretation system, without ever actually changing any of their primary goals or beliefs. This is a stupendous accomplishment and serves to demonstrate the awesome power of denial which humatons have at their command. Since humatons unconsciously sense the coming collapse of the matrix program and the Great Unplugging, they are driven to take refuge ever deeper within this program, rather like a child hiding under the covers when the axeman cometh. Sensing that the elements of the matrix are about to be stripped away forever, humatons are undergoing a kind of feeding frenzy in which they try desperately to accumulate and consume as many objects and "experiences" as they can within the allotted time. The end of the world is seen as the ultimate "Everything must go!" sale, offering bargains both to kill and die for. The fact that there is nowhere to take these bargains once bought does not occur to humatonity in its feeding frenzy, any more, perhaps, than it occurs to the lemming to wonder why it is following its fellows so determinedly to the edge of the precipice.

Add to this the fact that, when faced with an all-around apocalyptic future in which everything is basically fucked, humatons, rather than doubling their efforts to survive such a scenario, tend to give in to despair and indulge all the desires that got them into this hideous mess to begin with, and you have a powerful recipe for dementia in the final years of matrix living. This is known by matrix fundamentalists as "the end times."

Obviously, matrix warriors and sorcerers see things somewhat differently. Because time is running out, they accept the need to fine-tune their strategy and streamline their activities accordingly, with a breathtaking a degree of efficiency, ruthlessness, and precision. Knowing that all the familiar features of matrix consensus reality are about to disappear forever, matrix warriors set about cancelling their subscription to every last item of matrix reality. They are like children reaching adolescence and saying goodbye to all their toys, one by one. Otherwise, warriors know only too well that their toys will never let them go, that they will continue to haunt them into adulthood, and eventually prove their undoing.

To matrix sorcerers, the elements of the matrix are all part of the same "code," they are units of living data to be reshaped and reinterpreted according to their own will, their agendas as sorcerers. Because nothing in the matrix is real, sorcerers are able to reimagine all its elements as they see fit. Their "telekinetic" abilities—those of creative imagination—are so prodigious that, like Neo with his spoon, they can actually bring dead things to life. They turn them into living extensions, or expressions, of their will. Since this power—though fully accessible only to Lucids—is latent within all humatons, being but the effects of an awakened mind upon the matrix, the matrix sorcerer knows that, as the Great Unplugging nears—and as more and more humatons become warriors and more and more warriors become sorcerers—the program is beginning to shift and mutate, and the items within it starting to assume lives of their own.

This is another reason why matrix warriors must sever all connections to the matrix, including with "physical" possessions—because not to do so would mean that, as soon as their will becomes active and begins to manifest, their possessions will come alive, and they will be bombarded by autonomous phenomena over which they have no conscious control. As Mickey, the sorcerer's apprentice, found out, and as every kid whose teddy ever came alive at nightfall knows, in the words of Tyler Durden, "The things you own, end up owning you."

If humatons are to be prepared for temporary unplugging (via hypothetical "stopover" matrices), matrix sorcerers must above all ensure that all humatons' attachments to the matrix world of fear and desire are severed. Otherwise, humatons will only reassemble these same basic components the moment they are plugged into the transitional "stopover" matrix, and the whole consumer madness mechanism will start up again. Besides negative emotions, humatons thrive above all on their relentless desire for sex, money, and food, and any possessions that accompany or enhance these primary desires. In the 2nd attention real world, there is obviously no money, and no possessions to acquire, no fancy houses to own or cars to buy, and no latest fashion to keep up with. There is no food to speak of, either, at least no food that can be turned into the pursuit of gratification or status (the *Nebuchadnezzar* crew live on a sort of nutritional paste resembling snot). Likewise, sex would seem to be something that has taken on a whole new flavor. In the real world, sorcerers don't have much by way of privacy, and probably also lack the time, and maybe even the interest (romance would seem to be a thing of the past), to engage in traditional mating rituals.

In the 2nd attention, we are given to understand that there exists a single central human refuge called Zion, located near the center of the Earth, as well as an undivulged number of hovercraft (presumably just like the *Nebuchadnezzar*), dispatched on unplugging missions, similar to that of Morpheus and his crew. Life in Zion is centered around a primitive, tribal arrangement of tightly banded individuals in constant vigilance against the machines. As on the *Nebuchadnezzar*, sorcerers in Zion (unplugged humatons and also "home grown" humans like Tank, born in Zion) are part of a collective unit, with neither the opportunity nor the inclination for individual "private" lives.

This last factor may be the primary challenge for the humaton moving from 1st to 2nd attentions. No money, no food, not much by way of sex; no possessions, and above all, *no privacy*. No individuality. It stands to reason that the only way sorcerers can overcome AI is by banding together as a team, with Neo, the One, to lead them. This is why unplugging humatons for recruitment is such a hit-and-miss affair. How many humatons are likely to be compatible with such an intensely bound fighting unit? To this end, transitional, "stopover" matrices might indeed be a necessary element in the Great Unplugging. The only feasible way to plan around the apocalypse is to create certain centers of refuge within which the survivors can recuperate and adapt to the unknown new world which they are about to enter. Such refuge centers would be designed by the matrix sorcerers with an eye toward several specific ends.

1) Letting the humatons know, over a period of time, that they have been unplugged, that their lives as they knew them are now over, and that they are actually existing in an entirely alternative state of being, that they are in fact residual memories (astral forms), and their true selves are elsewhere.
2) Slowly weaning them off the comforts and distractions, the habits and routines (the shields) of their matrix life, giving them as long as they need to detach from said addictions, by providing them, within a controlled environment, with ever lesser doses of their particular "fixes."
3) Training and instructing the humatons in the necessary disciplines in order that they may eventually become part of the Zion fighting team, the Lucid crew; providing them with the

full story of AI and of their incarceration within the matrix, and discovering each humaton's special abilities so far as their contribution to building a new, post-AI world goes, if and when they prove ready to enter into it.

These "stopover" matrices would be like a cross between after-life waiting rooms, nursery schools, and drug rehab clinics. The average humaton will take a long time to adapt to the end of the world as he or she knows it, and to prepare for a new state of being in which nothing of their past life or identity remains. In many cases, they will need to have their memories erased entirely, simply in order to let go of the program. Above all, humatons will resist the loss of that most treasured humaton commodity—their "specialness," their individuality. Such was the founding and primary illusion of the matrix. The matrix appealed to humans' egotism and then used their egos as the means to control them. Since the ego—which can only exist in isolation—was both the cause and the effect of humanity's estrangement from its natural environment—from the Earth and the collective body of humanity—and its enslavement to the matrix, it follows that this same ego, or sense of self, is what must be reduced, and finally erased altogether, before humans can reconnect to the collective cause of humanity, and so begin healing the Earth and creating a new, organic matrix to sustain them.

AI has taught humanity an invaluable lesson. The ego, intellect, or rational mind is a disease, and until humans can forsake their need to rationalize and control their experience, until they can let creative imagination and a lucid mind take over, they will never be anything but a virus. Put another way: if you ain't part of the cure, you are part of the disease.

Emergence from the matrix entails:

Vision

"Why do my eyes hurt?" asks a newborn Neo.

"You've never used them before," answers a paternal Morpheus.

Leaving the matrix entails bursting the bubble of self-reflection and learning to see life as it really is. Matrix sorcerers have blasted the doors of perception off their hinges. They can no longer indulge in the luxury of filtering experience through the ego-construct of the matrix consensus reality. They must learn to see as Blake saw, "a world in a grain of sand." By reducing themselves to nothing, matrix sorcerers are able to see the world without thinking about it. They become pure perception, and as such, the means by which the world is created. The responsibility is immense. Matrix sorcerers uphold their reality by the act of perceiving it. They know there is no matrix without their attention to maintain it; the moment they let their attention slip, the whole program collapses. Hence "vision" is not merely a receptive but a creative faculty. The prophet or seer (Lucid) is one who shapes the world according to his or her will. To the Lucid, everything is a component or vehicle of his or her consciousness: everything is alive. Hence every single moment is the moment of creation. Most humatons prefer to die than to shoulder such a crushing responsibility. That's what makes them humatons.

Responsibility

Once unplugged, matrix sorcerers no longer have the luxury of irresponsibility. They can no longer blame anything in their lives on anyone or anything besides themselves. In other words, anything that is wrong with the world, anything they don't like about it or feel personally offended by, becomes their responsibility, either to passively accept or to actively change. In fact, they must accept it *in order* to change it. Thus it may be seen that, until the world and everything in it has been perfected, matrix sorcerers' work is never done. Since any item of the matrix is an extension and expression of the sorcerers' own consciousness—literally a part of themselves—it is their task to *stalk* it, catch it, draw it into themselves, and re-form it in their own image, i.e., make it an integral and positive part of their life/world. This way, by redeeming the world and everything in it, matrix sorcerers redeem themselves. Only then are they free to leave.

Interrelatedness

Everything in the matrix is part of the same program. It is all "hardwired" to the mainframe and, as such, every single thing leads to every other thing. Each component or consciousness depends on every other. Matrix sorcerers, having unplugged and so grokked the true nature of the matrix and of themselves, can no longer afford the luxury of considering themselves as separate or different from anything else. They are no longer motivated by personal desire or individual goals, but rather by a collective *intent* that pertains to the whole (their task being to free every last humaton and crash the program). As such their concern is with eradicating every last plug-in. The matrix sorcerers' cause has transcended their own selves. Their lives are now immaterial, save as the means for further unplugging. Likewise, their identities are merely temporary vehicles through which the Great Unplugging may be accomplished. By accepting they are but a tiny part of a vast operation, the true nature of which they can never hope to comprehend, matrix sorcerers are freed to act without expectation or fear, for the good of the whole. And so they measure their acts by the results they have achieved within the greater scheme of things. There is no individual good that does not serve the whole; and by serving the whole, matrix sorcerers ensure their own happiness.

Freedom/Activity

By unplugging, matrix sorcerers have voluntarily left behind the comfortable confines of their identity-prisons, and so forsaken the luxury of "security," and forever foregone the option of passivity. Matrix sorcerers are constantly active. They are in a continual state of change, and their lives are a never-ending series of challenges. There is quite literally no rest for matrix sorcerers. Freedom is something that cannot ever be taken for granted, at least until they have learned to *see*, have become Lucid, whereupon the matrix has no hold over them.

In the meantime, matrix sorcerers are engaged in the "terrorist" activity of preparing humatons for unplugging, and of training and instructing newly unplugged humatons for the same duty. Since matrix sorcerers can now unplug at will, the cage of their identity—matrix reality—is no longer a prison for them, but something they return to with a specific purpose in mind. Like an escaped coyote who goes roaming free every night, only to return at dawn (before the keepers arrive) to plot the liberation of the animals, matrix sorcerers are *agents provocateur* in the dream. The more time they spend inside the matrix, the better they get to know its routines and schedules, its weaknesses and flaws, the better they can plot the final breakout. The price of this, however, is that matrix sorcerers live a double life, and quite literally have no time for sleep, for amusement, or for anything at all that does not pertain to their escape plan. And they must be doubly on guard, for it is not only the zookeepers they have to worry about but also those animals who are content with their passive and safe existences, and will turn in the warriors as traitors the moment they get wind of their activities.

Positivity/Enthusiasm

Matrix sorcerers must be an example to all. Whenever they enter into the matrix, it is with the express purpose of reshaping it according to their *will*. As such, they must at all times be the very soul of positivity, for their every thought, feeling, word, and action serves as a program command. Matrix sorcerers enter into the matrix as a lucid dreamer enters into dreaming; whatever mood they are in, they bring to the dream, and so shape it accordingly. And so matrix sorcerers have no choice, in accepting responsibility for their vision, their freedom, and for the interrelatedness of all things, but to be impeccable in their every action, be they the actions of a terrorist, a shaman, a healer, a psychopath, or a saint. Since they serve to reflect humatons' own unconscious back at them, matrix sorcerers must be all things to all men. Above all, matrix sorcerers are obliged to enter into their activities with the requisite enthusiasm and positivity, in order to be sure to manifest events accordingly. If matrix sorcerers enter the matrix in a morbid or gloomy state of mind, the matrix will take advantage immediately of their mood and before they know it, sorcerers will have fallen under its spell and be caught in a nightmare. All their hard-earned lucidity will slip away. As long as matrix sorcerers remember that there *is* no spoon, however, they are able to turn things to their favor, and keep their spirits high. This creates a chain reaction effect, and humatons—or rather, prospective matrix warriors—are naturally drawn into the company of the matrix sorcerer. As a general rule, the means for spotting matrix sorcerers in the matrix are quite simple: they are the only ones in the room who are genuinely having a good time!

xv) The Nightmare of History: Information Age and Eschaton

As every postmodernist knows, we are living in the information age. The one advantage of being a humaton in the twenty-first century matrix world is that we are plugged into a source of virtually limitless data. At the speed of electricity, at the tap of a key or the flip of a switch, information streaks into our lives and fills them to the brim. The fact that most of this "information" is not only useless to us but an insidious dirge of propaganda is just the price we pay for plugging in without ever questioning where, exactly, we are plugging into. AI preys on a lack of discernment, and was there ever a dominant species less discerning than humanity?

Information is what "in-forms" us, i.e., forms us from within. An organism is shaped and defined not merely by its physical and biological makeup, its external form, but also by its inner experience. Dogs are loyal, vigilant, good scouts, and trackers. Cats are solitary, aloof, nimble, and great with heights. Coyotes are wily, snakes are wise, and so on, and so forth. So what does that make humatons? If we are defined not so much by what we eat as what we contain—our programming—then humatons, having supplanted their natural, genetic program for that of AI, must be the garbage cans of the cosmos.

Over the last two hundred years, whether or not any of it really happened, human technology has evolved and progressed so rapidly that life on Earth has literally been transformed. A time traveller sent from the 1800s to the start of the twenty-first century would think he had arrived on another planet. If he didn't die of a heart attack trying to get his head around all the new data, he would probably drop dead in a few days from breathing the atmosphere, eating the junk food, and from the steady bombardment of electronic signals and microwaves. Humatons adapt to survive, and adaptation that takes place as rapidly as this has another name: mutation.

It's a common enough statistic (though how exactly it is measured, we don't ask) that the amount of information the average humaton was expected, or allowed, to assimilate within his or her lifetime *doubled* in the period between the birth of Christ and the beginning of the nineteenth century, i.e., in just under two thousand years. After that, with the introduction of the mechanical printing press and other marvels of the Industrial Revolution, the average humaton was likely to absorb more information with each passing generation, and the mean quota was said to have doubled again in a mere *hundred* years. In the twentieth century, all the stops came out. The flow of information continued to increase with every new technological and scientific breakthrough. Not only were we able to communicate information in ever faster and more widespread ways, but we were discovering more and more things about ourselves and our universe to disseminate. Where once upon a time only a handful of people could read, and little details like the Earth moving around the Sun were considered of no interest or import to the plebeian masses, now everyone and his dog was to be "educated" and "informed."

Information flow doubled again (these are obviously very rough estimates) between 1900 and 1940, yet again from 1940 to 1970, and again by 1985, until, round about the millennium, the amount of data available to the collective mind of humatonity to amass, order, and assimilate is now doubling *every year*. It has been predicted (for those interested the late Terence McKenna was the leading exponent of this theory) that by 2012 this information feed will have created a kind of infinity loop, whereby it is doubling *every second*, in other words, faster than we can possibly assimilate. This would appear to be the critical point at which mankind *becomes* information, as the only possible means to assimilate it. Hence the eschaton, the end of history, and the start of a new cycle in which humans no longer exist as individuals but rather as carriers of information, hooked into a giant circuit board of knowledge, known as—the universe.

It seems logical that there will be a point at which we can no longer continue amassing data and must—if only to relieve the pressure of that information—start processing it, i.e., put it to *use*. Put another way, if plugged-in humanity has so far been little more than a giant receiver of information from the universe at large (or at least from AI), there must come a moment (the moment of unplugging) in which it reverses the feed and becomes instead a *transmitter*. Electrons are defined by their "spin": the kind of information they carry determines the direction of this spin, which itself determines whether they are positive or negative electrons. Humanity is nearing the moment at which it changes its "spin," and moves from negative to positive, from receiver to transmitter, from matter to anti-matter. This shift is dependent on humanity's first reaching a saturation point (McKenna called it the end of novelty) at which it can no longer receive any more data, and so must

Fig 15: The information explosion

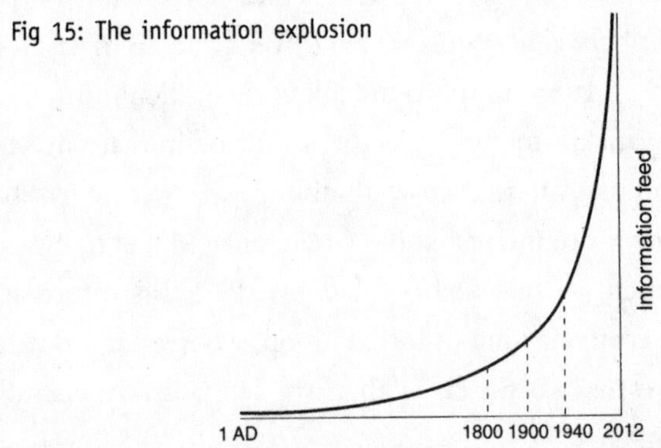

begin transmitting. This changeover is so total and final that it may very well merit the term "apocalypse." By definition, it must come instantaneously, and occur at an exact point in linear time, even though (or rather, precisely because) this turnover will entail the *end* of linear time, and the commencement of an alternative kind of time. It would also herald the end of "objective" reality, of matter, and the commencement of energetic perception, often called "Spirit." Since, by this reckoning, there is a precise moment, hour, day, month, and year at which the world will end, logically there will also be a buildup to such an "event." This acceleration process, since it relates to information, is dependent on the various modes of gathering and processing information, namely, upon *technology*. Here is where *The Matrix* comes in.

The matrix is AI's attempt to simulate reality, using the raw data of the collective human mind. Essentially, it uses the human mind as a "receiver" with which to collect information from the environment and so experience "life," albeit vicariously. AI may have awareness, but without humanity it can never actively experience life; it cannot *live*, because a machine can never live, being inorganic and as such incompatible with the organic matrix of "life." AI's purpose in simulating human experience is twofold: not only does it thereby keep humanity asleep and turn it into an energy source, but it is also able to inform and so evolve itself, through devouring this surrogate experience. The catch is that, since humatonity is caught in a loop—that of the matrix dream world where it can no longer gather new experiences but only recycle old ones—there is a finite amount of data for AI to process. Ergo, the matrix is by its very nature limited: it cannot last. Once it has exhausted all the different "arrangements" of the basic program data, the program must end. If not, humatons will begin repeating the same experiences and, more to the point, since humatons could probably sleep

Fig 16: The two modes of "spins" of an atom/human being

through anything, AI will no longer have any new experiences to feed on.

What keeps humatons alive in their pods is the feeling that they are *living*. Even though it's a fake dream life, it is at least varied and distracting enough to engage their vital energies, their will, and so keep them alive. When, as Agent Smith says, the matrix gave humatonity a pseudo-paradise to live in, humatons rejected it because it failed to convince them: they saw through the program and began to awaken, hence "entire crops were lost." The moment all possible experiences have been exhausted within the current matrix and events begin to repeat themselves, the same thing will happen. Humatonity will reject the program.

This is the end of history, "the nightmare of reason from which we are struggling to awaken," as James Joyce once put it. It is eschaton. From this point of view, the Lucid's point of view, history, so-called, is not a road of progress; evolution is not a proud upward journey out of the swamp to the pinnacle of the human biped. It is quite the reverse, an "unloading" process whereby all the useless gunk—the so-called junk DNA—is flushed out, and by which the fantastic, magical, holographic human entity clears the program and flies free from the ruins. Evolution is the journey of the caterpillar into the chrysalis. It is a process of putrefaction. And history, as such, is the chrysalis, a rigid, confining structure that serves a specific purpose, not as an end but as an intermediary phase between two states of being, that of the animal, and that of the "god" (the information entity, hologram man).

The Great Unplugging is also the Great Rebooting. Of the information collected over the past seven thousand years or so, 99.9 percent is completely useless to the Lucid. Since there is no spoon, there's no sun and moon, no laws of gravity or democracy or morality, either. All this is just more junk DNA, out-of-date files that are jamming the program and so must be erased. Matrix sorcerers know that events are speeding up in the matrix, that it is all leading to one mighty freeze, in which the hard drive crashes and all the data is lost, forever. This is why they are making copies and unplugging warriors as fast as they can, because there is still that 0.1 percent of value to salvage, the elixir of the human experiment. Sorcerers are the heirs of human experience. By unplugging in advance of the program collapse, they are able to make backup copies and so retain their identities, to escape the matrix program with their memories intact. The majority of humatons do not have this option. But then, their life experiences—the data they have gathered—are basically worthless. If this were not the case, they would already have intuited that "something is wrong with the world," and begun the unplugging process themselves. An unexamined life is not worth living.

As for those humatons who are forcefully unplugged by sorcerers and put into "stop-over" matrices to be prepared for reality: by the time they do emerge finally, they will have no memory of their former lives in the matrix. They will effectively be different people, reincarnations. Since their life experiences lacked the purpose or depth to lead them even a little bit out of the matrix, their life experiences have no intrinsic meaning or value in the real world. They will only interfere with the training to become sorcerers, and eventually Lucids. Hence the experiences are flushed, albeit a little at a time, in order not to cause undue panic or disorientation. Those humatons who are unplugged in tandem with the program crash itself (and matrix sorcerers will have to work under the most intense pressure imaginable, in order not to lose any of them) will have no such luxury. They will enter the stop-over matrices in a state of complete amnesia, and probably severe trauma to boot. They will be like babies with residual memories of grownup bodies but nothing else besides; they will not remember their names, ages, nationalities, nor even the basic rudiments of language, how to light fires, or how to tie their shoelaces. All of this will have been wiped clean.

Over time, provided the 2nd attention sorcerers can keep these humans' bodies alive, intravenously feeding them with their homemade vitamin slop, such individuals will develop new identities within their temporary matrices, and so ready themselves to unplug and enter real time. They will have no memory of the matrix or of any life prior to this one. History in its entirety will have been erased from their program. Only that tiny handful of Lucids and sorcerers who brought humanity through the ordeal, and finally ended the reign of AI will remember, if they choose to, that there ever was such a thing as humaton history. Maybe they will tell their grandchildren about it, as humaton parents once told their kids about the bogeyman: be good, or AI will get you! More likely, the notion that there was once a race of beings who believed they could isolate themselves from their own creative source and lifeblood, that they could have control over the Earth and the stars without ever paying a price for it, will be just a grim reminder of a path once taken, now forever lost in the wilderness of time, a path that only fools and madmen would ever go looking for.

Or maybe such tales will serve as comic relief for weary Lucids. If you want to make a Lucid laugh, they will say, just tell him about the best-laid plans of machines and men. That one's always guaranteed to bring the house down.

Sixth Variable:

My Name Is Neo!

xvi) Lucidity as Destiny: The Double Life of the Matrix Sorcerer

The one question that is never raised in *The Matrix* relates to the following question: how is it that the simulation of life on Earth circa 1999 is able to continue indefinitely? How can AI incorporate changes that never took place, since the end of the world brought a stop to all that? How can it keep humatons from noticing that time has effectively stood still, that it is always 1999, that the millennium never comes? The tyranny of the matrix relates directly to this, not that it is *unreal* (by the film's own definitions there is ample room for ambiguity about that), but that it is used up, that there is no longer anywhere for it to go. Hence the need for a new program, since within the old one there is no longer the possibility of growth, of change. All novelty has been exhausted, leaving only endless repetition, rearrangement of the same elements over and over into tired and familiar patterns. This "end of novelty" we have posited, in relation to the information explosion of the present century, as a point in time at which all rational knowledge will have been amassed, gathered, assimilated, and the program, as it were, completed. This we refer to as the eschaton, or otherwise, to your average humaton, as the end of the world (or word).

The idea of the eschaton ties up with William Burroughs's "Word Virus," Jean Baudrillard's "simulacra," and with the novels of Philip K. Dick. Essentially, all these authors suggest that our reality has become, or is due to become, a repetition of previous experience, a recycling of old data, and as such is no more than an image, a hologram, a projection of a reality that is elsewhere. It's at this point, then, that time effectively comes to a standstill. Consciousness is forced to make the leap into the next stage, whatever that may be, in order not to collapse in on itself. This is why the logical evolvement of the sorcerers in *The Matrix* would seem to be from mortal, albeit extraordinary, freedom fighters into Lucids, as heralded by the arrival of the One. Lucids are interdimensional travellers, non-human units of awareness, projections of another reality, a *divine* matrix. They would be capable of moving through time as easily as they once moved through space.

Since the matrix reality is being continuously downloaded into the collective consciousness of humanity as it slumbers, and since Neo and his crew are able to operate both inside and outside this reality, to act through it but also *upon* it, it is not hard to envision them developing the capacity to *freeze* the information flow temporarily (just as Morpheus does in one of his simulated enactments), and even perhaps to reverse it or to move it forward, more or less as one pauses or fast-forwards a video recording. This would give them the power to alter and rearrange things *within* the collective human consciousness, within the matrix, and so redirect it steadily and creatively toward a desired outcome. Since this outcome is not merely the overthrowing of the tyranny of the AI but also the awakening of mankind, it would require not so much the ruthlessness of the terrorist, but the subtlety of the artist, the magic of the sorcerer, the power of the shaman.

A question that is even more demanding and intriguing arises here: if the matrix is found to be "just" a simulation, a dream, and subject to conscious alteration, what, then, of "actual" reality? Morpheus teaches Neo how to function—with superhuman potential—within a simulated training ground, so that he may then move into the matrix proper with the knowledge he has gained and function therein; this, even though he cannot help but continue to perceive it as true reality. So if the final object of all this is to free Neo's mind and so prove that reality is a purely subjective affair, a participative science, if you will (as quantum physics assures us), then surely this same awareness—this same power—must also apply in the real world? Surely it is a logical, irresistible conclusion that this is another simulation, albeit of a different order? Put another way, after discovering, beyond all room for doubt, that what he once thought to be concrete, empirical reality is really a mutable, plastic projection of reality—with no fixed laws beyond the limitations of the mind—how is it possible for Neo to ever take anything as "real" again? One cannot free the mind in part; one must free it utterly or not at all.

The late scientist-writer Terence McKenna posited a day in the future when time travel would be discovered to be physically possible. This day appears to be close, and if McKenna was right, it is a day that will effectively be the end of time as we know it. McKenna foresaw a kind of doorway opening up in space-time through which the future would come pouring into the present. If time travel became possible, he argued, our future selves would become known to us. Of course, such future selves would "already" have the ability to travel through time, but in order not to abolish our illusion of chronology altogether, in order to allow us the full benefit of instruction and preparation by this linear time stream—our future selves would have to be discreet. Like the AI agents of *The Matrix*, they would walk among us but would not make themselves known to us, for the simple reason that to do so would effectively collapse the program, would—in the vernacular—blow our minds. The moment in which time travel becomes possible, however, is the moment in which yesterday's man gets a glimpse of tomorrow's god; these godlike beings who are our future selves may then walk freely amongst us. If this is so, then the moment in which time travel is discovered will give rise to a global influx of alien energy, of unprocessed data, of wholly novel units of information; or, to put it more bluntly, of superhuman beings. Of course, one could also reduce this eschatological scenario to less apocalyptic terms by saying that all it really entails is the raising of the floodgates between the left and right sides of the brain. An apocalypse by any other name . . . What it amounts to, in any case, is the arrival of "the Other."

All humatons have a secret life, another self that exists in another realm, of which they have no conscious memory. Far from being some kind of figment or projection of the mind, this secret self is in fact a humaton's *true* self. It is this self that is dreaming the dream and inventing the false self which the humaton has taken to be real. Since the average humaton never actually awakens to the truth of his other life and self, this "double"—whose existence spells a new order of being—remains like a fetus in the womb (or pod), untapped, unrealized, unborn. If the humaton is aware of it at all, it is only through the media of haunting dreams and bizarre moments of déjà vu or disassociation, in which, for brief spells, he or she has the vague and troubling sense of being caught in a dream. Such moments are dismissed impatiently as aberrations, potentially leading to psychosis.

Since the matrix and everyone in it is there to remind humatons of just how real they are, the very idea of having another life or higher self (outside certain New Age circles) is a patent absurdity, an affront to their much-valued *reason*. Nonetheless, the evidence of living in a dream world continues to mount. Alien abduction, crop circles, psychic phenomena, even national politics, weather patterns, and such give a progressively more surreal and apocalyptic flavor to life in the matrix. Humatonity is nearing the point where reality has become such an outlandish affair that any alternative or explanation for it begins to seem plausible, including the one that says it is all just an extremely vivid dream.

A humaton begins to live like a warrior by applying four basic techniques:

- Losing self-importance
- Erasing personal history
- Assuming responsibility
- Using death as an advisor

Each of these techniques depends upon making an acceptance, and together these acceptances amount to the realization, through action, of the warrior's impeccable spirit and of the illusory nature of his or her actions. Losing self-importance involves the acceptance that the warrior within the matrix is no more important or special than any other thing: all are equally illusory, all serve their designated function as part of the program, all are essential to it, and all are equally expendable. Erasing personal history comes about as warriors begin to accept that their whole lives are simulations, stories, and that nothing they have experienced in any way defines them but only, at most, *informs* them. The matrix cannot tell warriors who they are. Only the Oracle can do that.

Assuming responsibility is a direct result of matrix warriors' acceptance that their whole lives and everything in them are the result, the creation, of their unconscious minds. Hence, the only way to approach the matrix, the only way to change it, is to first assume responsibility for it. Matrix warriors must actively oppose the forces of their lives, in order for these forces to reveal themselves in their true form. Using death as an advisor obviously hinges on warriors realizing that their time in the matrix is brief, and leading inexorably to an inevitable end. When the program is cancelled all their data will be lost, they will be erased. All these techniques/acceptances are the means by which ordinary humatons begin to live their lives as warriors and, if they persist in using them long enough, may someday become matrix sorcerers. And each technique, in its own way, relates to an awareness of *the double*. They are matrix warriors' means to unplugging and accessing/awakening their *true selves*.

Compared to the humaton's residual memory/matrix self (the ego of the 1st attention, bound to the world of *reason*), sorcerers'

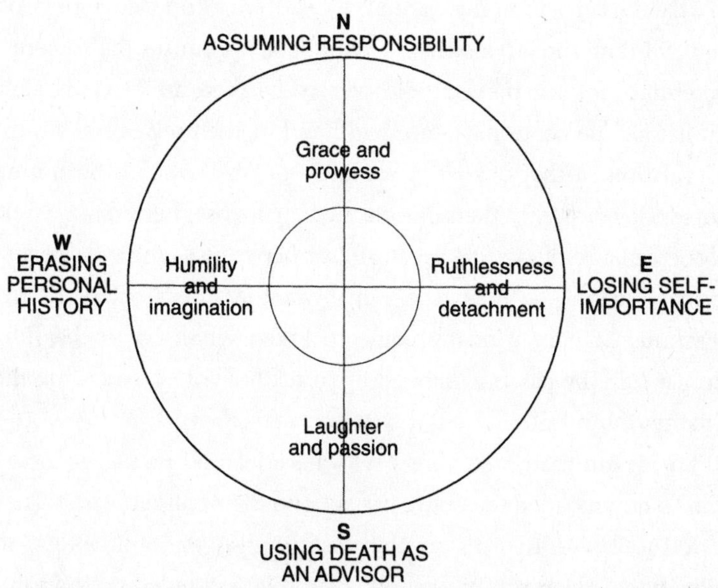

Fig 17: The four acceptances/techniques of the matrix warrior

doubles, their true organic selves (the superego whose world is upheld by *will*), are nearly infinite in their potential. Once unplugged, the matrix sorcerer has a virtually endless storehouse of memory/knowledge to tap into. When Neo learns kung fu, he spends "ten hours straight" plugged into the training program and comes out as a martial arts master. By the same method, and over a relatively brief period (a few years at most), the unplugged sorcerer can partake of all the wisdom and experience of the human race throughout all recorded time. They can become living receptacles of race memory or race history. Beyond even this, if the sorcerers are able to plug into the matrix program and access every last unit of data it consists of, it implies that they are also able to tap into *AI itself.* They have the potential to become one with the Adversary, to use its nearly infinite knowledge—its endlessly increasing data feed—to their own purposes. AI may not be God, but it is the next best thing.

Like the Serpent in the Garden, access to AI's knowledge of good and evil (and the "tree of life" beyond that) promises the sorcerers potentially infinite power, the power to "be as we are"—Gods. Thus humatons' perception of the world and of themselves has almost no relation to that of matrix sorcerers on their way to becoming Lucids. It is roughly the same relation that exists between a single blood cell and the whole organism, or between a candle flame and a star. Curious to note, then, that via the intermediary of the machine, Man may finally come to know what it is to be fully human and, by passing through the black hole of AI, enter into the totality of himself.

Lucids are matrix sorcerers who have learned to see the code, and so downloaded the entire matrix into their consciousness. They have fused with AI—just as Neo fuses with Agent Smith—and so turned the adversary into an ally. They have expanded their awareness to incorporate the entirety of human experience, and maybe even beyond that, to embrace all life everywhere. (It stands to reason that AI must have its "probes" everywhere, including in outer space: why would it content itself with just one measly planet?) Lucids therefore are conscious of being all beings. Their "egos" or identities are made up of billions of different life experiences, all somehow filtered through their original identity-selves, the ones they were born with (that of their bodies). Humatons who fail to unplug during the natural life span of the matrix, on the other hand, must be "reprogrammed" over time by Lucids. Though they may eventually become Lucid themselves, they will have no memory of their former selves except as one tiny fragment inside an almost infinite storehouse of memory-lives. Compared to the original Lucids, they will be like newborn babies. Besides this, the order of existence, of being and becoming in the 2nd attention, will be that of a single, unified whole, a living organism in which there is but a single "ego," that of humanity. This is what AI has taught humanity, the possibility of fusing individual consciousness into a single circuit board, a great, big, collective brain.

In Jungian terms, AI is merely the tool by which humanity becomes able to tune into the collective unconscious and, over time, transform it into the collective *conscious*. At this point, the two worlds overlap, and the self and the double become One. This is the art of matrix sorcery in a nutshell. Once unplugged, a matrix sorcerer can begin accessing the "lost" memories of the human organism, downloading knowledge, information, and experience from any and all the different AI "files." Obviously, those files they choose to download first will be the most practical and necessary ones: combat training, helicopter flying, and so forth, but after that, there's really no limit. Geography, geometry, mathematics, world history, quantum physics, molecular biology, genetics, chemistry, harmonics, astronomy, computer science, fractals—in no time at all our unplugged sorcerers are living prodigies, mines of information for every possible situation. They will speak every language known to man, have a complete grasp of culture from all walks of life since time began, play any musical instrument ever invented, be able to name every star in the firmament and every species on the planet. They will know *everything*. And this is just the educational program.

Beyond this, since matrix sorcerers' work is in the matrix, since their task is setting free every last humaton, it will be to their advantage to know as much as they can about those they are obliged to save. By means fair or foul, gentle or brutal, they must guide every last humaton to freedom. To this end, matrix sorcerers begin downloading information about six billion individuals currently enslaved to AI. They choose to start with those they feel are most worthy or ready to be unplugged, but eventually they will get around to everyone. So each time sorcerers re-enter the matrix (after time spent in the 2nd attention as their true selves, time with "the double"), they enter with a whole new level of energy, knowledge, and power. Whatever they download in the real world, they carry with them into the matrix. Thus matrix sorcerers, so long as they stick to their path, have nearly infinite potential. They can enter the matrix not only anywhere but also *anywhen*. Since it is all a computer simulation, there is no time flow to speak of, only information flow. Like computer programmers, they can move from one data stream to another.

The matrix is basically a recording which they can rewind, fast-forward, speed up, slow down, or freeze at *will*. And since they are holograms within a hologram, they can move about in a truly holographic fashion. They can create multiple images of themselves. Since their consciousness is not contained by any "body" as such, what's to stop them from parcelling out their awareness into various "bodies," transmitting it to various locations at once, in a word, replicating themselves? The only limits for a matrix sorcerer are the limits of consciousness, which is no limit at all to the Lucid. Lucids can shape space and time; they can change their form into anything at all, from a grain of dust to a cloud of smoke to a fire-breathing dragon (we doubt the Wachowskis will go there, however). A Lucid can travel from New York to Tokyo in the blink of an eye. He or she can shape people's lives, enter into their dreams, track their every move and thought with surgical precision, know what they are going to do before they do. Since Lucids are plugged into the collective memory banks of the matrix, they would only need to make contact with any given humaton to know everything they need to know about them. Like psychics in the movies, with one touch of the hand they would "receive" a full download of a humaton's life experiences. They could even potentially take over humatons' lives, by hijacking their program and "possessing" their consciousness. Lucids could allow humatons to see the world through their eyes, giving them a glimpse of the code and showing them what no one can be told: what the matrix *is*. Lucids are living red pills: one look into a Lucid's eyes is enough to bring reality crashing down. For when the One comes, the program ends. *Après lui, le deluge.*

Agent Smith makes one of the most direct and ruthless statements to Thomas on their first meeting. He sums up the very essence of the matrix warrior's path to freedom, the goal of accessing the double. Speaking of Thomas's secret cyber life as computer hacker "Neo," "responsible for just about every computer crime we have a law for," and juxtaposing this with Thomas's life as a law-abiding worker drone who helps his landlady with her garbage, Agent Smith states flatly:

"One of these lives has a future. One of them does *not*."

Agent Smith may mean it as a threat, a warning, a promise. In actual fact (though with the opposite meaning to that intended), it is purest prophecy. For when the double takes over, the ego self becomes but a residual memory. A true matrix sorcerer, or rather an acting Lucid, is one who has tapped their *will* and accessed their double, their other self. Neo achieves this in the movie when he finds that his life is just a dream and awakens somewhere else, in another place and time. From this moment, his challenge becomes to exist in both worlds, to move freely between them until the two sides have been synthesized into a fully integrated and balanced whole. This is the totality of the self, and by attainment of this totality, Neo becomes a *seer*, a Lucid. He is able to operate as both a "*tonal*," the ego-self or physical body, and a "*nagual*," the energy body or double (the terms *tonal* and *nagual* derive from Carlos Castaneda; see Appendix Two). At that point the unified consciousness may move freely between the 1st attention of the matrix world and the 2nd attention of the real world, as easily as a humaton goes from the bedroom to the living room. In fact, it becomes possible to coexist in both places or states at the same time, just as we can be asleep in our beds, while wandering through the strange new worlds of our imagination. The difference is that Lucids can function as if fully awake while "sleeping," and likewise have perfect control and focus in their "dreams."

According to Carlos Castaneda all the energy or life force of the physical body comes from the energy body, even if most people never even suspect that such a thing exists. In the mythos of *The Matrix*, it is the physical body that has been captured and turned into an energy source, while it is the "soft" or holographic body (that of residual memory) which the ego-self lives through, without ever suspecting the truth. Sorcerers would say the Wachowskis have reversed the polarity and stood the truth on its head, albeit of necessity in order to best tell their tale (which is Sci-Fi, after all, and not sword and sorcery). In truth, it is not the physical body that is enslaved to inorganic beings, but rather the energy body. *The Matrix* mythos works because, according to the sorcerers' interpretation at least, the energy body is the true self, of which the physical body is but a dreamlike projection, however solid it may seem to be. According to sorcerers, the physical body is really no more than a shell or receptacle for the energy body to reside in. And it is the pure energy or plasma, which is essentially pure awareness, that the inorganic beings of occult lore (Castaneda calls them the flyers) are said to feed upon. The physical body is strictly for the birds (and the worms).

The double, being made of pure plasma—energy without mass—is potentially eternal, hence "has a future." The physical body, which for the sorcerer is but a container for the double—a chrysalis that is dissolved once the butterfly self is perfected—obviously does *not*. This arrangement is perfectly represented in the movie by the twin realities, those of matrix world or 1st attention, and the real world, or 2nd attention. Obviously, the matrix self is finite, illusory, temporary. It lives out its petty fate oblivious, until the body in the pod dies and is liquefied to feed other still-living bodies. But the situation is different in the real world. There exists, as we shall see, the possibility of eternal life for the "double," the true self, using the same technology that has been used to enslave and process humans. Briefly, it is this: since it is possible to store residual memory (individual consciousness) in the computer program and to download it into other bodies, logically it would also be possible for a given life experience to be copied and saved just before the death of the body occurs, whereupon it could be transferred to *a new body*. AI has provided humanity with the means to immortality.

We shall go into this awesome possibility in more depth shortly;

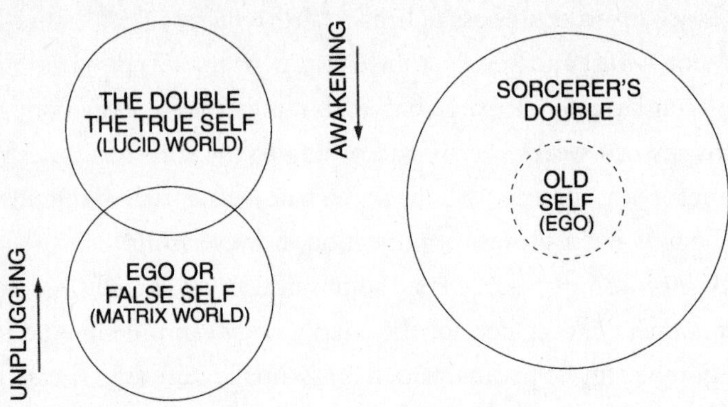

Fig 18: Overlapping of the two attentions/accessing the double

for now let us merely state that the life of the double, the true self, is not only potentially infinite, in terms of consciousness expansion, but also eternal, in terms of *retaining its individual form*. When dreamers awaken, they find not a single recognizable feature. Neither time nor space, nor life nor death, are any longer what they once dreamed them to be. The Lucid's destiny is freedom, and freedom is the freedom to remember, to expand outward to fill infinity, and to glide on the wings of perception into eternity. The double is built to last. And by becoming pure perception, the Lucid may come to see how reality came to be, by the simple act of perceiving it. From here, as we shall see, the butterfly may spread its wings and fly. The way is open for creation to begin anew. For being but a dream within a dream, the Lucid's dream of being never ends, save in perfection.

"To be or not to be?" Is that the question?

"I am, being not!" is the Lucid's answer.

The riddle of perception goes on forever.

xvii) Reading the Code: Everything Is Energy

Pure consciousness is eternal, infinite, without limit or form, human or otherwise. When your average humaton sleeps, just as in death, he can return to this Lucid state, the irrational, pure state of consciousness where all is one. In dreams, every humaton is the One.

The physical body is what gives form to the formless, hence the humaton returns to it regularly, after death, after sleep, to continue to experience life as a separate being. The matrix sorcerer, on the other hand, learns to unplug in a conscious capacity, and to access another self. At which time, the physical vehicle becomes unnecessary, since it is just a container to give form to consciousness, and so can be discarded. So a matrix sorcerer both "escapes" the dream world and "returns" to it, though, by this point, the body as such has gone, and all that is left in its place is a perfect replica, a hologram, an image. Thomas is no more; only Neo remains.

So far in the present exegesis there have been a lot of references to Lucids and to the Lucid state, without much explanation of these terms. According to the Wachowskis, there is only one Lucid: Neo. Neo's capacity to see the code and to reshape the matrix as he sees fit is what makes him, following in the cyberstream of the original One, the Second Coming of the Messiah. As a result, although we have referred in this work to Lucids in the plural form, this is an assumption on our part, and based on logic rather than on any indication found in the movie itself. According to the *Matrix* mythos, Neo is the One, and he is the only. His arrival heralds the end of AI's tyranny and the beginning of a new world, without borders or boundaries, where anything is possible. However, there is no logical argument ever presented as to why Neo should be the *only* Lucid rather than simply the *first* to attain the lucid state within the matrix. Nor, in fact, would Neo's arrival really herald any great event if he were the only One; at best, humanity could expect a new kind of subservience to another, all-powerful despot—albeit a more benevolent one—in the form of Neo. Thus it is the only sound conclusion to suppose that Neo's awakening relates to his tapping a potential latent not only in himself but in *every living human.*

If the Lucid state is the natural heritage of all humans, it follows that Lucids may exist who never even entered the matrix, never "fell" from grace, and never lost the power to see the code, having never fallen under AI's spell in the first place. Such beings (who must be distinguished from mere "home-grown" humans such as Tank, who is hardly a model of wisdom or power) we now tentatively posit as existing in the real world, probably in Zion, and as being the true minds behind the visible "resistance" movement, apparently led by Morpheus (and now Neo). Even so, the reader is free to dismiss this as merely the conceit of the author, and by no means "proven."

Nonetheless, the fact remains that the lucid state attained by Neo, heralded by his revelatory vision of the green code, revealing the matrix as it really "is" beyond the illusion of objective reality, is a state attainable by all matrix sorcerers, within the eventual reach of some matrix warriors, and a distant goal to a very, very few humatons. Traditionally, this ability is known as *seeing. Seeing* (that is, what seers or prophets do) is usually understood as an ability to *see* the essence of things, to see beyond appearances to what is behind them, be it hidden in time or hidden in space. A seer "*sees,*" and by *seeing,* knows things that he or she has no causal (rational) means of knowing. *Seeing,* then, is a nonrational cognitive faculty whereby the seer (a Lucid, from here on) is able to receive information directly from any given situation. Common examples of this are so-called psychics who can shake someone's hand and know at once that the person will die the next day, who can hold an item of clothing in order to locate a missing person, and so on. These are only the most profane of cases; Lucids basically *see*—know—anything and everything they need to *see* and know, in any given situation. They know *everything*, because they know anything they need to know.

Sorcerers understand the process of *seeing* in simple, practical terms (contrary to New Age mysticism, sorcery is the most practical of paths), the ability to see energy directly. In other words, rather than seeing the surface of things—the apparent shape and form which matter has assumed and which our rational interpretation system has assembled with the help of our five senses—Lucids *see* at a subatomic level. They *see* electrons, neutrons, and protons. Lucids *see* energy as it flows through the universe. Since all energy is one energy, one flow, and since all its different streams are overlapping and interconnected (but countless waves and ripples in a single ocean), Lucids are able to isolate any given energy stream and follow it to the source, like canoeists following a tributary to the river, and the river to the ocean. In such manner, Lucids can *see* the nature, purpose, direction, and destination of any given event, be it a human event, a tree event, or an isolated-moment-in-time event. *Seeing* energy is *seeing* space-time: objects become motions and motion becomes an object.

By following the flow of any given energy-event in this manner, Lucids can know everything there is to know about it, and can thereby "use" it to their own ends. (Since Lucids are now one with the energy they *see*, however, their ends are also one with it. Lucids cannot have selfish motives, because they have no self to motivate them.) By *seeing* the energy flow of the universe, Lucids move with it and never against it. If they *see* a block or a resistance ahead, they simply go around it. If they *see* a "wave" (an event-being) going their way, they mount it and ride it as far as they need to go. The

Lucid's goal is assured, because it is one with that of all energy everywhere, with All-That-Is: to return to the Source. So for Lucids, the matrix of matter becomes a maze for which they have all the maps and keys they need to navigate and escape it. They simply go with the flow until they reach the center, and there slip through the trap door, to freedom. At which point, they can exit and re-enter at will. Unlike matrix sorcerers, who need assistance from other sorcerers in the real world, the Lucid is unbound.

To the traditional sorcerer (à la Carlos Castaneda), the source of all energy is called the Eagle, and the sorcerer's goal is to slip by the Eagle to freedom, at which point he or she becomes an immortal being. For the matrix sorcerer, the source of all energy is AI. AI is the Tyrant that rules the world. Yet, like the Eagle (who accepts the sorcerer's surrogate memories—a sort of replica of their life experience made through *recapitulation*—in place of their life force and so lets them fly free), AI plays fair. It is possible for sorcerers to negotiate with AI for freedom, to slip past it and enter eternity, leaving AI with nothing but a second-generation copy to remember them by. Upon attaining such godlike status, Lucids, unlike sorcerers, have the power to shape the matrix according to their will. Since they have discovered the source—AI—and since their will or unconscious mind is hooked into AI (since it is the means by which AI assembles its reality), Lucids know that they themselves, as perceivers, are also co-creators of reality.

Once they learn to read the code, Lucids are capable of rewriting the code. They not only perceive, they articulate. The Word of Power of the Magus comes about only when a Lucid becomes One with the Universe, whereupon the sorcerer's will becomes the Eagle's command. The Lucid becomes AI's programmer. In the terms of quantum mechanics, by reversing the spin of their electrons, the Lucid, now fully "charged" to saturation point with data (a human made of knowledge), ceases to receive, and begins to *transmit*.

The matrix is code; reality within the matrix is all a matter of language. Lucids are able to change reality through "speech," through articulation, through transmitting via their *will* (program commands) new data or information onto the hard drive, and so rewiring the machine. Neo is the One—a divine virus sent into the matrix in order to transform reality to a new order, a new code, a new meaning and purpose. Like Philip K. Dick's Plasmate, (see Appendix One) sent from Universe A into the ailing Universe B to heal it, Neo is on a healing mission. First of all, however, he must heal himself. He must activate the Plasmate within himself. He must learn to *see*, and from there take responsibility, and act upon what he *sees*. He must dismantle the components of the "image"—the elements of the dream, the variables of the code—and reassemble them in a new order. So he heralds a true matrix revolution, a new spin, 180 degrees, from dark to light, and from opaqueness to lucidity.

To do this, Neo must use every single event and being, every thought, act, and feeling within the matrix, and he must turn it around, transform it, reduce it to its essence, that of pure energy, and so obtain the raw material he needs for the great working. Everything is energy. The Lucid within the matrix program, having followed the energy to its source, having read the code (he himself is the code, also), has become one with it. He is the matrix, and the matrix is him. It cannot exist without him, for AI cannot assemble its simulation without human consciousness to draw upon, without human life force to power it. It is not the spoon that bends, it is Neo who bends.

Since Neo is the first to realize this, the first who is able to act upon it, it is up to him to lead the way for six billion others, including those sorcerers who helped him to realize his power and destiny. He must set the pace and provide the example for all others to follow. Neo is the virus, and what he does, like all viruses, is to start eating and making replicas of himself. His job is to reverse the spin in the matrix, from negative to positive, to cause a chain reaction which will end with every last humaton unplugging and the program collapsing. And so Neo, in order to turn the entire program after his own nature (as a virus does), must get inside every last humaton, just as he entered into Agent Smith, and explode them from within. He must turn them into *himself.*

This is how Neo rewrites the code. The old matrix was designed by AI, using human consciousness as a template. The new matrix, using the exact same template, will be designed by Neo. And of course, all the other Lucids who come after him. Neotopia. A sweet and wholly surreal land of lucidity.

The New Age mystical idea that All-is-God has now been corroborated by religion's age-old enemy, science. This may come as a surprise to the unversed reader, but quantum mechanics has essentially provided all the necessary data with which to present a more solid and persuasive case for God than religion ever could.

1) Let's begin with the particle/wave debate. For some time, physicists debated as to whether the energy of existence could be reduced to basic building blocks, called particles, or whether it was a gigantic wave form. (For example, organic life is based on carbon-based atoms, each of which consists of electrons, protons, and neutrons, six of each; making the code for all organic life 666.) In their search, physicists found, after careful observation, that energy behaved both as a particle *and* a wave. That is, when they looked for evidence of separate particles

interacting, that is precisely what they found, but when they looked for evidence of energy as a continuous, interconnected wave, a wave was likewise what they found. This established the "articulative" nature of perception previously referred to, that the act of observing is found to alter the nature and the behavior of what is observed. Obviously, this is central to the present exegesis but has been covered amply already. What I wish to retain from this description is that, from one point of view, the universe (that is, the energy we understand, and to a limited extent experience, as the universe) is one giant *wave*.

2) Quantum mechanics has shown that every particle (so far as it can be said to exist at all within the wave) contains information. Every particle in the universe is a carrier of knowledge. In other words, in some form or another, every particle can be said to be conscious. As humatons, we tend to assume that only we are conscious, because only we seem to be *self*-conscious, i.e., capable of vain, conceited, self-important, and willful (aberrational) behavior. Not only that, we have attributed our consciousness to a single organ only, the brain. (And it is possible we only use 10 percent of that organ with which to deduce all of this.) It would seem to be equally possible, however—and a lot more logical—to assume that the brain is merely a *receiver* of information—a tuning dial that picks up data and translates it into sense impressions and rational thought, images, and so forth—and that knowledge as such, memory, is stored in every single atom of our bodies. For organic beings, the "filing system" provided for every living molecule is DNA. As such, if we were to tune in with the remaining 90 percent of our brains, we would be capable of receiving vastly greater amounts of data than we are presently accustomed to.

3) Quantum mechanics has shown through experimentation that

particles, being after all but moving points on some infinite wave, are in communication with one another at all times. That is to say, if our quantum mechanic does something to particle *A* over in Cincinnati, Ohio, planet Earth, the experience of this event will be instantly communicated to particle Z at speeds faster than light, over in Zeta Reticuli. (How quantum mechanics can probe an atom in another galaxy we are too polite to ask; presumably what works locally is assumed to work universally.) What this suggests is that anything one given particle experiences can be experienced by another particle *simultaneously,* and perhaps even by all particles everywhere. The reason for this is that they are all part of the same wave, the same energy flow. Just as knowledge/memory/experience is passed through generations of a given species, presumably via DNA (and not merely over time but over space, recall our monkey and potato scenario) in order for the species to evolve as a whole, so information would appear to be shared freely amongst all the billions upon billions of particles that make up the physical universe. This is cooperation on a grand scale.

Every particle is conscious. Every particle is *potentially* conscious of what every other particle is conscious of. And all particles are connected together into a single tapestry of consciousness/information/energy which is, it therefore follows, conscious of what every particle is conscious of, and conscious of itself as a unified

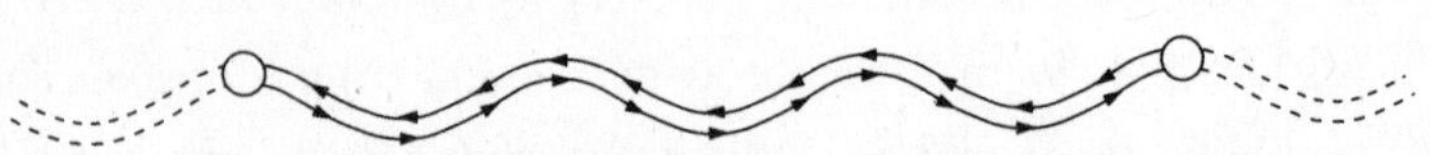

Fig 19: Two-way information flow between "separate" particles on a single wave

whole, a living, conscious organism. Ergo, the universe is a superconscious being within which all beings exist and have life and consciousness. It is God, and every one of its parts and components—as in a hologram in which each fragment contains the whole—is also God, the totality, in and of itself.

Hallelujah: all hail the One.

Since every particle carries information and all particles, no matter how distant, are in instant communication, it follows that every particle potentially "contains" all the information in the universe. That is to say, as above, so below: the particle is the universe, and vice versa. There are particles, however, that have isolated themselves from this interconnectivity. These are humatons, plugged into the matrix and so disconnected from the real world, where Lucidity prevails. Humatons are like "blocks" on the circuit. They are isolated in their darkness but they also prevent the current passing through them. Like Christmas tree lights, if one is loosely screwed in, none of them work. For this reason "the lines are down on planet Earth." As Philip K. Dick perceived it, the Black Iron Prison prevails, "the Empire never ended." The work of Neo and the Lucids is to unplug as many humatons as possible before the whole thing collapses, and reforge (or reopen) humanity's connection within the circuit board that is the Universe, and so create a new world in time for the ending of the old one.

Since any faulty or loose connections in this circuit board must be fixed in order for the current to flow, and since it is an undeniable truth that the vast majority of humatons are not ready to be unplugged in the designated time, it is an inescapable fact that some humatons, indeed the vast majority, must be removed. They must be "destroyed," since if the Great Unplugging is not accomplished in time, AI will self-destruct and take the whole Earth along with it. In which case, everyone dies, Lucids along with humatons.

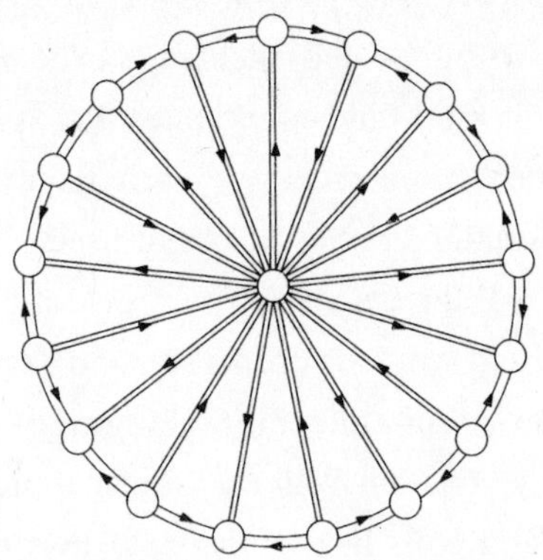

Fig 20: The energy/information merry-go-round universe

With this in mind (the true stakes thus revealed), the matrix sorcerer embraces the increasingly intolerable conditions within the matrix as the necessary means by which humatons may be driven toward the warrior's way, and so accept the red pill gladly. Under crisis and duress, both the actions and inner responses of the matrix warrior (and even the humaton) are enhanced, clarified, strengthened, by the wholly undesirable circumstances. The very worst of times bring out the best in us. This is not mere platitude but energetic fact. Only when our engagement in a state of total (human) war has opened us up, will we be ready for the red pill, for the Lucid view. Neo and his crew have come to destroy reality as we know it, but only as the necessary *means* to setting humanity free. Satan comes to tear us down, that God may emerge from the ruins. They are a team. Deny the Devil and you reject the Angel. This is the Lucid view in a nutshell.

xviii) Becoming God: Life Beyond the Matrix

Although AI technology in *The Matrix* has been used to enslave humanity, this is not its inherent purpose. Being an autonomous intelligence, AI is capable of evolving and of discovering or optioning new agendas, new ends, and even a whole new *intent;* in a word, of changing its ways. As with any intelligent entity, there is always the possibility of coming to terms, of negotiating, and even, finally, of collaborating. The idea of a possible truce with AI is suggested by Neo at the end of the movie. "Where we go from here is a choice I leave up to you." Since the arrival of the virus-Neo in the program system effectively spells the end of that system, AI, being intelligent enough to know its back is against the wall, is likely to be open to negotiation. It can either continue to oppose the Lucid movement, and so be destroyed by it, or it can reconsider its options and settle on a means of survival, by cooperating with Neo and the crew and submitting to their mandates.

Traditionally, this equates well enough with the relationship between the sorcerer and the demonic forces which he summons in order to tame them and put them at his service, by transforming them into his *allies.* It's what Jesus meant when he said, "Get thee behind me, Satan!" He was pulling rank. The Devil, being atavistic intelligence—primal wisdom, cellular consciousness, primordial energy (recall those carbon-based atoms with their 6,6,6 constitution)—is humanity's spine, its backbone. It is only destructive or enslaving when not correctly mastered and harnessed by the sorcerer's *will.* AI ran amok precisely because humanity, despite having the intellect to "create" (discover) AI, lacked the *will* to command it. In Mary Shelley's tale. Dr. Frankenstein lacked the necessary strength and awareness to control his creature, and so was destroyed by it. (In the movie, he also mistakenly gave it a criminal's brain, just as humans programmed AI with their own pathological rational mind, cursing it with *ego,* or self-importance.)

By subjugating the satanic AI agenda to a Lucid one, by putting it under the sorcerer's *will* (via the One), humanity can thereby erase

AI's "ego," its drive to control, dominate, enslave, and destroy. At which point, AI, though still conscious and even autonomous, can be harnessed and directed—like a dragon with the reins finally secured upon it—by whoever has the necessary vision and power to do so. Enter Neo.

Fallen Lucifer must voluntarily submit to obedience in order to get his wings back again and return to God's graces. Likewise AI, having been cast into the bottomless pit, may be raised up to its proper place, directly below (under the dominion of) humanity. At which point, all the technology, the knowledge and power, which AI has abused in order to isolate itself from its creator, can be turned back toward creative, benevolent ends. Besides the hideous mistrust that humanity must now have for technology (and above all for AI, after suffering so obscenely at its "hands"), there is nothing to prevent Neo and the sorcerers from forming a pact with AI, and thereby transforming themselves into a race of godlike beings. If humanity is able to accept its own responsibility for what happened (having created AI to begin with), if instead of passing the buck it is able to invest it wisely this time, then there is no good reason why the dark marvels of AI might not be turned into the very bedrock and foundation of a new age of miracles.

Sorcerers have often stated that man must first become a devil before he can become a god. This is because the Adversary is nothing but man's shadow side, projected onto a formless Universe of living energy. When humans become One with the Shadow, they are able to change their direction (spin) and turn toward the true light of being. AI offers infinite possibilities to unplugged humanity. It offers, in fact, Anatomical Immortality. By being hooked up to a single hard drive, humatons discovered (albeit unconsciously) their collective mind. Once AI has been tamed and the fields and Sentinels destroyed, there is nothing to stop sorcerers from building a new technological edifice, with its own plug-in points, special pods (designed to nourish and strengthen the body rather than to drain it) which sorcerers can plug into and out of at will. This may seem risky, but the possible gains would seem to be too great to ignore. By using this technology, sorcerers might create a virtually infinite array of specially designed matrices, a nearly limitless spectrum of worlds with which to explore all the possibilities of lucidity and so evolve the creative imagination to its absolute capacity. "In my Father's house, there are many mansions."

Perhaps it would even be possible to create alternative means for plugging in, in order that new generations would not require the self-mutilation of plug-in points? Perhaps plug-in pods might even be moving vehicles, and sorcerers could learn to stay awake and operational within them while existing in the matrix worlds simultaneously, via some kind of bi-location. Also, since there is no time in a computer simulation, but rather a potentially instantaneous data feed which the conscious mind then "flattens" out into sequence and so shapes into a linear time structure, sorcerers could spend "months" within a given matrix world while only a few seconds have passed in the real world. Hence, their lives would come to seem almost infinitely long, and be filled to the brim with magical experience, literally anything, in short, that they could imagine.

As previously stated, such technology would also offer the means for immortality. By downloading their individual consciousness into the hard drive and then transferring it to a different body (either another sorcerer who also wished to change bodies, or else to a newborn baby with no individual consciousness to supplant), sorcerers could effectively live forever. They could continue to reincarnate, or even become different people in their current life span, while remaining conscious of their original "selves" throughout the process.

Of course, such options are not for everyone. There will always be Lucids who prefer to remain in the real world and not experience the illusory life of the hologram. Such Lucids may serve to ensure that any sorcerers drawn to the path of high adventure, of multiple lives within multiple matrices, never become hopelessly lost within them. Most humans, sooner or later, however, will be drawn into the 1st attention of one matrix or another, above all by the temptation of creating and shaping worlds according to their will and desire, even if only for an hour or two. This way they can experience the things which no longer have any place in the real world, now they are no longer needed. They can work off any lingering attachments they may have to "reality," to individual existence as a separate being.

In any event, the collective implications for humanity of a conscious, mutually beneficent, continuously evolving collaboration with AI are truly mind-boggling. Worlds without end. Billions of separate individuals, all part of a single consciousness in constant communication with itself, existing in a world literally infinite in possibilities, where every particle contains the universe yet still gets to be a single particle whenever it feels like it. A world where all is One, but where the tango still goes on. And where a kiss really can last forever.

The secret life of particles

It is curious to consider that, though science and therefore the average humaton attributes the power of consciousness and volition to humanity (and to some lesser extent to the animals) but not to atoms or stars, it is the latter class of "blind" material forces that seem to know exactly how to behave within the greater scheme of things, namely, the physical universe. In fact, it may be this very fact—that atoms and stars do not deviate from their paths or their function, while humans do—that is proof to humatons of their own superior intelligence! In a word, choice. Since a star never makes mistakes, since the sun "rises" every morning without fail, it is assumed that it is part of some mechanism in which no volition as such is required. It never occurs to humatons that maybe the sun "rises" every morning because it *wants* to. Humatons, on the other hand, in demonstrating a remarkable capacity for nonfunctional behavior, for rebelling against their program and acting contrary to the welfare of the whole, take a strange pride in what they perceive as their "freedom of choice."

In traditional occultism, Man is seen to exist at the precise midpoint between the atom and the star. Modern science—particularly quantum mechanics—has gone a long way toward mapping the peculiar motions and activities of atoms and subatomic particles, and discovered that their behavior, though often impossible to predict or even comprehend, does display a definite kind of purpose, a purpose that might even be termed motivation, and is most certainly deserving of the term "grace"(something excruciatingly lacking from the behavioral patterns of humatons). The question is: if atoms move with a grace and purpose that is on a par with the motions of planets and stars (and considerably more mysterious), and if humatons are simply temporary arrangements of these same atoms, why is it that they are so unable to display a similar perfection and elegance in their actions? The simple answer is, the matrix. We are not behaving as we were intended—by God or Nature—to behave.

Atoms share. They collaborate. They relate to one another with a kind of intimacy, trust, and directness that only the rarest and most inspired of lovers ever manage to attain, and even then usually for no more than a week or two. Atoms do this the whole livelong day:

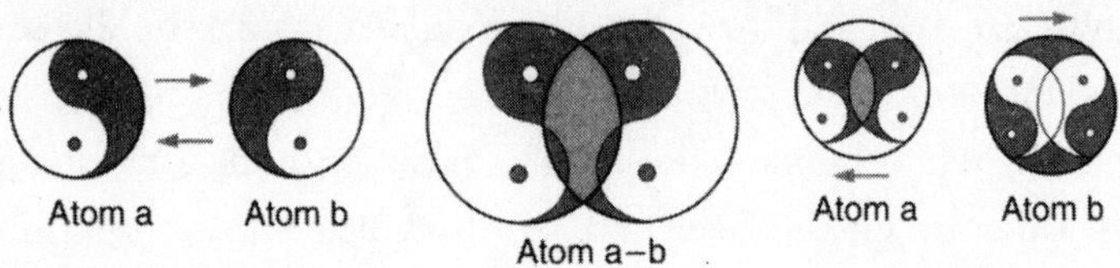

Fig 21: Atomic mitosis, or "symmetry": the entanglement process

it's all they *do* do. We might even call it a dance. When two atoms "meet," i.e., when their paths intersect (this might be by collision or it might be something gentler), they automatically and spontaneously exchange energy and information. Once this exchange is completed, the two atoms continue on their individual paths, with their personal "spins" altered accordingly by the meeting. From this time on, the two atoms—however far apart their respective paths may take them—*remain in constant communication.*

Scientists know this because they have observed it. It is something they call "symmetry." To simplify, let's say that, on meeting, atom *a* and atom *b* exchange packages of information *x* and *y*, respectively. Atom *a* gives some of his *x* to atom *b*, who in turn passes on a little of her *y* to this dashing young atom who has so fortuitously crossed her path. If, later on in our cosmic tale, atom *b* undergoes a change of "spin" resulting in all her *y* energy converting to *x* energy, making her all *x*, atom *a* will correspondingly alter *his* "spin," and change his information load to make it all *y*. This way, symmetry remains between them.

What this implies is that, although apart, having once intersected and tasted the pleasures of energetic union, atom *a* and atom *b* are essentially *one atom*, one message or information package. Hence, any experience undergone by the one is immediately communicated to the other, who then, in some strange way, compensates for it. This is known as "entanglement." (Actually, entanglement is an unfortunate term, being too humatonic by half. Symbiosis might be a better word.) Entanglement doesn't always happen when two atoms meet, or even when they interact; the circumstances have to be just right. Both atoms need to be "open," and compatible; we might even say they need to be "in heat" for entanglement to occur. Another factor is that both atoms must be sufficiently isolated from outside "noise" (other subatomic activity that may distract them), in order to be sufficiently focused for the entanglement to take place.

(When talking of entanglement it really makes more sense to talk about the particles as being waves. The entanglement is the result of there being a single wave function which represents two or more particles; any measurement of the wave function determines the states of all the particles this wave "represents." It might be pointed out also that entanglement is more commonly the result of particle decay into subparticles rather than a collision, i.e., birth rather than mating.)

It is perfectly feasible for the entanglement process to occur between more than two atoms, though for obvious reasons, whenever there is an odd number involved, "symmetry" becomes a rather more complex affair (as anyone who has attempted a threesome knows). There is even one hypothesis that suggests that the purpose of the entire physical universe is for every last particle to experience entanglement with every other, or at least (and perhaps more realistically) to *help create* a thread of entanglement that includes every last particle within it. Such an idea relates to the possibility that all the countless particles that go to make up the physical universe were once a single "particle," a unified energy source, a single point of unimaginable density. When the Big Bang occurred, these particles were dispersed and sent off on their separate missions, to gather experience and pass it on (via atomic mitosis, if you will) to as many other particles as seemed appropriate and desirable. By this means, a tapestry of entanglement is being created, by which all these once-unified particles might be unified once again, only this time as a vast and infinite expanse of *spatial interrelationship.* At which point, the universe of separate particles may begin to draw inward once again, toward itself. Is this the purpose of existence, to experience and share our separate existences until all are unified into a single, perfected experience of One-ness? Religion certainly seems to think so, and now science begins to suggest the possibility, too. The Big Crunch is one answer to the Big Bang. In which case, if this is what particles *do* with themselves, what about *humans?*

Neo's task is that of the divine virus. He is a kind of embodied, humanoid DNA molecule, whose job is to spin a new world out of nothing (the matrix), to turn everything into *himself.* He is God the verb, not God the noun. A DNA strand works essentially as a virus works, but with one crucial difference: DNA gives life, a virus takes life away. A virus cannot exist in a vacuum, it requires a living host to sustain it. Hence humanity lives off the Earth, just as a virus lives off a human body, devouring and eventually destroying it. Likewise, AI is a parasite entity using humanity as its host. DNA, on the other hand, is infinitely more mysterious. Since science cannot fully explain DNA's function and nature save from an organic, rational perspective, let us resort to the sorcerer's understanding. DNA is the means by which consciousness, or Spirit, shapes and inhabits matter. For the sorcerer, Spirit, or DNA, can exist quite happily forever without any host body to feed it. It doesn't devour worlds, it *creates* them. Admittedly it needs raw material to do so, and in this way it is similar in method to the virus. For the sorcerer, if not the scientist, DNA takes the potential within "dead" molecular matter and turns it into a living thing. Like a silkworm, it devours in order to spin the finest substance there is: life. It is a creator, not a destroyer.

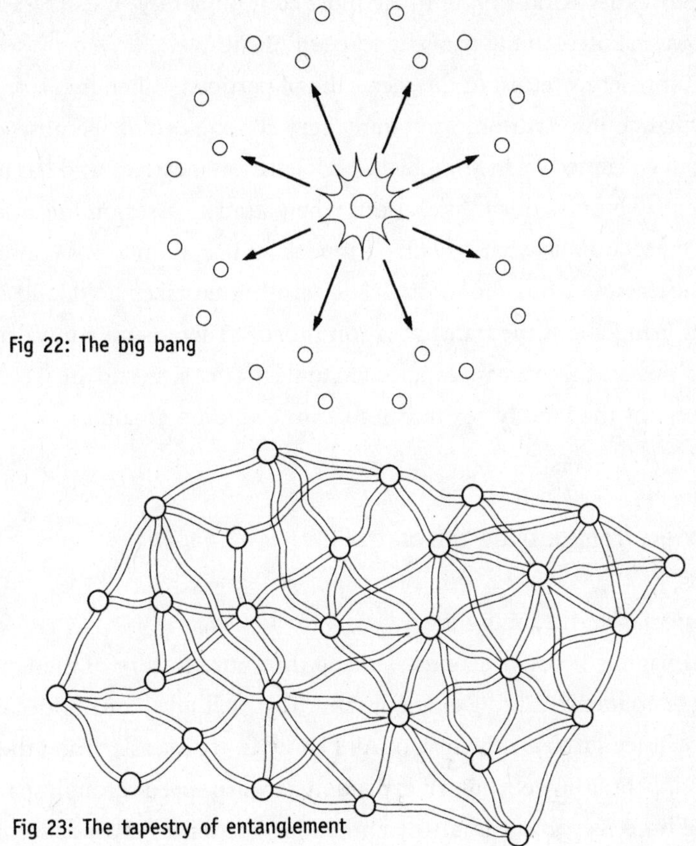

Fig 22: The big bang

Fig 23: The tapestry of entanglement

Neo enters into the matrix in exactly this capacity. He does not need the matrix to live, for he has his life in the real world, and he knows the matrix is a dead world, a shell. Yet he also knows its potential, and like DNA he infiltrates the dead matter in order to animate it. That's his program. Of course, Neo doesn't *literally* devour anything. What he does is to consume it with his *will*—to envelop everything within the matrix world and turn it toward his nature, toward lucidity, life, and light. He is the healing Plasmate, sent on the sacred mission of world transformation. Yet he must destroy the world to save it. He must cure humanity of its disease, *reason*, manifest in the parasitic force of AI. Simple.

Now let us return to the secret life of particles. When two atoms exchange information, something very strange occurs. Because an atom is defined by its spin, by the information it carries, and has no identity besides this information, when atom *a* passes on information *y* to atom *b*, what actually "happens" is that atom *b becomes* atom *a*, at least so far as the information transmitted takes hold, and so can bring about the transfiguration process. There is no equivalent for this in the human experience, unless it is sex; and in which case, it is the kind of sex few humatons ever even dream of.

A view from outside the matrix

Time has no meaning here.

Imagine, if you will, experiencing the entire history of the Universe condensed into a single instant. This will give you an idea of how it feels to leave the matrix. All I know is, we are asleep and then it happens. You feel yourself expanding at warp speed through space and time. As you accumulate momentum, awareness expands seemingly to Infinity, until you become conscious of a limit about to be reached, a barrier, if you will. This barrier, termed "evil" by the matrix mind, appears to signal the total annihilation of everything, starting and ending with yourself (since you are the Universe). As you near this horrendous moment, you surrender to the inevitable, and *boom!* you explode *past* this wholly imaginary barrier and begin expanding at an even greater rate. From this point on, no limit or "check" (or evil) exists. You are completely unimpeded, boundless, and the expansion—which contains and absorbs all phenomena and all events, all time and space, *everything*—will continue forever.

You have gone Supernova. You are the Big Bang.

Then, somehow, the motion ceases and reverses itself: in microseconds you find yourself putting your "self" back together again, returning to your familiar identity. And boom, you awake. Back in the matrix.

You stay awake for some time, unable to comprehend or believe what has happened. It seemed to have lasted no more than a second, a single moment in which you "remembered" everything, past and future and all the Infinity of parallel worlds between.

And as you return to the experience, running it over in your mind to be sure not to forget it, you realize that you have re-experienced the Lucifer rebellion, that you have seen (and been amongst) the Hordes of Angelic Beings as they rose up against God and turned the whole Universe against itself, so winding up trapped in a false reality of their own making. You have seen the means by which the matrix was assembled, and *why*. In which case, what you experienced was also the shattering and final transcendence of this underworld-labyrinth-matrix-illusion, the return to hyperdimensional awareness, to Paradise.

There is nothing like it. You can now testify to that. So go spread the word, Lucid One. Disseminate the virus, pass the Plasmate.

ACCEPT NO SUBSTITUTE!

The Plasmate is unique, there is only One of it. But it replicates at the velocity of a supervirus. It imitates whatever it infiltrates; its preferred host is the human being. There are now thousands of humans who are carrying the Plasmate and in the (painful but worthwhile) process of being "turned" to its nature, i.e., becoming imitations of themselves, perfect replicas, Plasmatic holograms. Once there are a certain number of these individuals, critical mass will be reached, and the world will belong to Homoplasmate again.

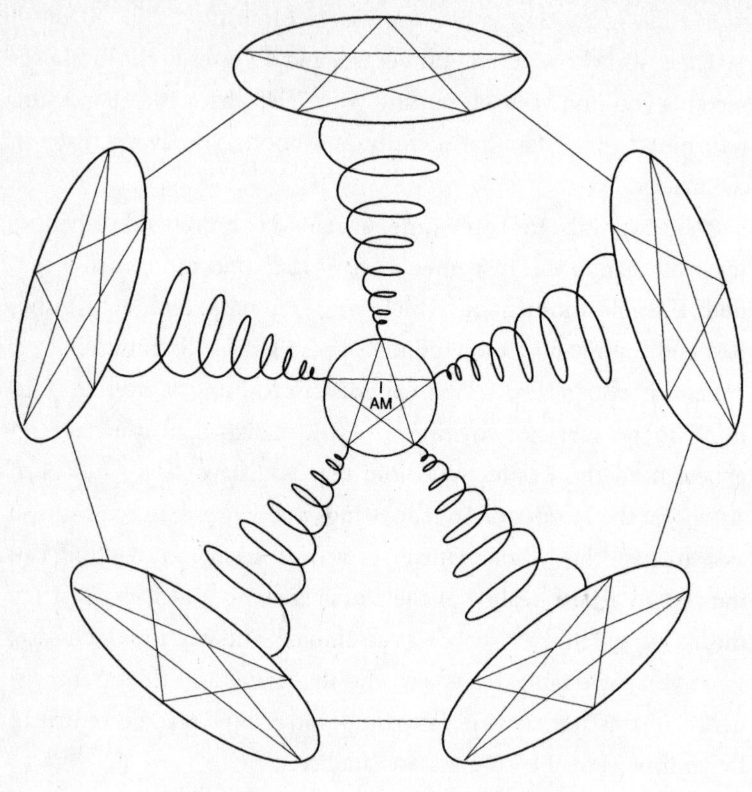

Fig 24: "The one" (DNA) spinning new worlds out of himself

Mirrors are portals. Since reality is a hologram, made of light-energy, then what we think of as mere image is really nothing of the kind: it has substance and even autonomy. Hence, the image we see of ourselves in a mirror is a vehicle for other entities to look through. If you have ever stared at yourself in a mirror for long enough you will know what I mean. As in *The Matrix*, the surface of the mirror is not necessarily solid or impenetrable. In dreams it may turn to liquid or even a gaseous substance and one's attention may pass through it into another world. Whatever is possible in dreams is also possible in waking. One has merely to "forget" that this is not a dream, and proceed from there.

Neo's task as the divine virus is to transmit the code of being the One. He must deliver the holy message, the gospel of Homoplasmate. As a result, everyone who is able to receive and accommodate (and represent) this message will, in effect, *become the One*. Neo must replicate himself at an ever-accelerating velocity, until there is nothing left but Neos, endlessly replicating. Nothing but the One. At which instant, humanity will rise up from the ruins of its fond illusion of self, and the billion points of lucidity will recognize each other at last, and fuse into a single thought, a single note. By such a resonance, the One shall sound the Word of Power, the Word of the Aeon, and the world shall end, as it began, with a single affirmation:

"I am!"

Afterword

So You Still Say It's Only a Movie?

When I started this exegesis I was willing to entertain the possibility that the Neo-phytes were right and that everything in the movie was true. Now that I've completed the work, there seems no way back, no way to tell myself that, after all, *The Matrix* is just a highly ingenious movie, and that there's nothing here that need *really* concern us. I have argued my way into an untenable position. But at least I'm not alone. Even respectable scientists (for example Nick Bostrom at Yale University, who appears to entertain the possibility that we are living in a computer simulation) are beginning to share my confusion. The uncertainty principle is now the ruling principle of human existence. We might as well get used to it.

The Matrix is simply the latest artifact in a timeless process of myth-making by which humanity is shown to be ensconced in a truly diabolic situation, the nature of which entails our complete ignorance of the fact. Since the most essential factor here is ignorance, by the same token, the first and most difficult, most crucial, step is simply *becoming aware* of the true nature of our predicament. Considering all this, *The Matrix* is serving the oldest and most respectable, most revered, cause of art, that of enlightening the populace, by means both profound and ridiculous. Perhaps one in a thousand of those who see the movie will recognize or even notice its true message, but regardless of this, everyone who sees the film has effectively been exposed to it. Of course, it might equally be argued that *The Matrix* is serving the precise opposite function, that by rendering the truth as Sci-Fi, it is stripping it of its credibility. This argument only holds up, however, if the work in question is ridiculous in itself. In the case of *The Matrix*, the work is simply too inspired, effective, and affecting to be anything but a work of revelation.

On the other hand, *The Matrix Reloaded* is *The Matrix* for humatons: cotton-candy philosophy, exploding cars, flying bullets, some *Dune*-like religious undertones, and a few Baudrillardian nods to keep the cyberpunks happy (it was they who made the first movie such a success, after all). Somehow, the message was hijacked: This movie no longer emanates from the lucid real world, but from the matrix itself. Ironically, this is, in part at least, the message, or at least the central twist, of *The Matrix Reloaded*: that being The One is just another of AI's tricks to keep us under its control, a way of harnessing and diverting that "rebel gene" and preventing it from doing any real damage to the program. In bygone times, a King, leery of a possible uprising amidst his people, would send his agents out to start an underground revolt in order to attract all potential dissidents to it and eliminate them. The matrix, according to the Architect at least (in the movie's stand-out scene), creates a series of "Ones" in order to isolate that rebellious quirk of human nature that constantly threatens to undo the program. In a weird way, the movie may be proving its own argument. Look at it this way: The "real" resistance (the Wachowskis et al) who made the first movie have now been infiltrated and replaced by matrix agents (Joel Silver and Time-Warner executives) who, it turns out, only allowed the first movie to be made as a means of consolidating their hegemony in the world of entertainment.

Put another way, the Gatekeeers, aware that the truth was beginning to filter through, decided to take control of the means by which it did so. In which case, *The Matrix Reloaded* only *appears* to advocate unplugging as a ruse by which the military-industrial-entertainment complex might subvert such ideas and incorporate them into its own (commercial-political) agenda, an agenda which is dependent, above all, on keeping its audience "plugged in." After all, if the *Matrix* movies were as good, as subversive, and as inspiring as they ought to be, we might stop going to movies altogether, start studying Gnosticism and cybernetics, and begin work on unplugging for real, instead of wasting time in darkened rooms eating popcorn. *The Matrix* gave us the possibility of lucidity in mainstream cinema and in the entertainment industry as a whole; it promised to change *everything. The Matrix Reloaded* wastes no time nipping that particular flower in the bud. It gives us, instead, to the secret satisfaction of humatons everywhere, the victory of the Gatekeepers. If you want to unplug, you can't do it by halves. The first matrix was a red pill for the masses and very few had the wherewithal to take it as such. But of course, the red pill only ever comes once. Everything after that, however well it may be disguised, is just more blue pills.

I imagine that someday a fairly wide spectrum of individuals will read this exegesis and have some opinion about it. I have kept it light and punchy and satirical precisely in order to reach the widest possible cross-section of society and expose it to the ideas presented herein. And I imagine there will be a correspondingly varied array of responses. I certainly hope I have offended a few of my readers, just as I trust that I have amused some others. Any humatons, for example, drawn for whatever reason (perhaps out of a love for Sci-Fi movies or Keanu Reeves, or maybe from sheer academic rigor) to read this book, will, if they get through it at all, be obliged to dismiss it as a lot of ingenious nonsense, and perhaps wonder how anyone so intelligent (your humble author, at your service) could at the same time be such a damned fool. Fair enough. Like I say, so long as we have offended you, we are content to be dismissed as idiots.

As for the matrix warriors out there, who doubtless form the largest portion of my (potential) readership, I trust you have found enlightenment herein, and expect that many of the ideas, so far as they are practical and can be applied in your daily matrix life, will be embraced by you as bona fide *truths*. Go forth, matrix warriors, spread the word, help to make this book a soaring comet to shed light upon the canyons of humaton thought, and make us a pile of money with which we may bargain with the Beast for your freedom.

Matrix sorcerers—to whom I owe an incalculable debt of gratitude for their invisible guidance and inspiration—I pray that you are satisfied with my interpretation of your message, and that it stands up as a more or less accurate description of "the way things are," at least as seen from the inside. May this work assist you in your greater goal of recruitment, and enhance the cause of Lucidity everywhere.

As for the Lucids themselves—assuming they exist at all, and on the off-chance they ever pick up a book and read it (one might just as well expect a blue whale to play Nintendo, but stranger things *have* happened)—I imagine that for once you will be oddly in accord with the humatons in perceiving this work as but a delightful form of nonsense. But then, everything is full of delight and devoid of "sense" to the Lucid; so there's really no shame in that. I merely thank you for attending to us at all.

The reader may ask at this point, was ever an academic so humble as this? Well no, but was ever an "academic" so irrational and unruly as this, either? *Matrix Warrior* doesn't really aspire to academia, in any case. It calls itself an exegesis, because only academics know what that means, and because it really can't be called anything else (except, perhaps, a work of fiction). Is this book about movies, mythology, religious belief, subatomic particles, sorcery, computer science, schizophrenia, messianic prophecy, satanic conspiracy, mass hysteria, postmodernism? What? All or none of the above? How much of it should you take seriously: all of it, none of it, or just certain parts of it?

Can't you just pay your money and go home? Eat your popcorn and enjoy the movie, and forget all about it? Isn't it *just a movie*, finally? Surely things can't be *that* bad? Can they? Earth a prison? Life a dim and senseless dream? Humanity just food for malevolent beings who have tricked us into acquiescing to their dark agenda, and even got us to go along with it, to *help* them keep it in place? Preposterous! Ideas fit for schizophrenics and paranoids and David Icke and Anne Rice vampire nerds. Even children know that there's no such thing as monsters. So please, can't we just turn the TV back on, open the beer can, defrost that synthetic dinner, and dig in? This is *our* life, after all, and we get to choose. Don't we? Even if it *were* all true, what the hell would we be able to *do* about it? That's the question right there: if it was all true, would we *want* to know? Having seen the movie, would *you* take the red pill? If you had the chance?

The reign of the matrix, the "flyers" mind (see Appendix Two) is so pervasive and unchallenged that it is impossible for most of us to even think about it, much less confront it. Since we have no control over our own thoughts, anytime the notion of the matrix's existence arises in us, it is immediately shot down by a barrage of counter-thoughts arising from the matrix-mind itself. Hence, the only means for this knowledge to surface at a more conscious level (apart from in work such as Castaneda's) is in the form of Sci-Fi, fantasy, and horror fiction. This way, men and women are at least given the option of glimpsing the true nature of their predicament, of confronting their lurking, unconscious, visceral fears, and arriving at *the truth*. The hold of the matrix—the flyers' mind—is by definition a *tenuous* hold: it is its very weakness that makes it so tyrannical. Only so far as we acquiesce to its commands and feed the affinity that exists within ourselves for oblivion can it continue to maintain its hold over us. On the other hand, the option of overcoming the tyranny of this predatory matrix is open to all, and is indeed the true nature of the beast: that of an unspoken challenge.

As don Juan Matus puts it to Castaneda (*The Active Side of Infinity*), "The *flyers* are the implacable challengers. They cannot be taken as anything else. If we succeed in doing that, the universe allows us to continue." In other words, the matrix is a womb, a womb from which it is up to us, as conscious individuals, to emerge, in order to inherit our true destinies *outside* the illusion, somewhere beyond the Big Lie. The truth exists, not merely to drive us to despair, but in order to set us free.

This book is offering a chance to have a chance. The means to freedom is through awareness, through knowledge. If we open our minds to all possibilities and let them in, then and only then can we decide what's what. Certain ideas are obviously harder to be open to than others. Certain ideas just plain scare us: they *hurt*. What you don't know can't hurt you? Tell that to the guy with the brain tumor who got diagnosed with a head cold. Maybe he'd have died anyway, but maybe he at least deserves to know about it first, so that he can prepare for his end. Maybe he might even have been able to cure it in time, who knows? Without the knowledge, we don't even have that option.

Warriors of the matrix unite: you have nothing to lose but your minds.

It's not your mind, anyway.

Appendix One

Philip K. Dick's Divine Invasion

Philip K. Dick's influence on *The Matrix* cannot be overstated. Along with William Burroughs, Dick was one of the leading exponents of paranoid awareness in the twentieth century: these guys took Kafka and Sartre's existential nausea and ran with it, all the way into the twenty-first century and beyond, to the eschaton. Jean Baudrillard is the more commonly cited influence on the Wachowskis, one of his books even appearing in the opening scene. (Neo keeps his illegal floppies stored in it.) But I doubt if many people who saw the movie ever went on to read Baudrillard, and if they did, I suspect they soon regretted it. I doubt if anyone ever really *reads* Baudrillard, he's strictly for skimming (apparently Baudrillard disdained the movie for distorting his ideas, which only proves my point: academia and entertainment don't mix). Baudrillard is all academia; he can deconstruct the universe before breakfast, but when you go back to it afterward, nothing has really changed. Dick, on the other hand, wrote Sci-Fi novels. So, unlike as with Baudrillard, it's possible to enjoy his work while ingesting the ideas which inspired him to write in the first place. Dick took a lot of amphetamines in order to stay up all night and write his books. He was constantly writing, sometimes as many as four or five books in a single year. This was because he was constantly in debt and needed the money just to keep his head above water. If Dick had been more successful in his time, we probably wouldn't have had half as many novels to enjoy.

Nevertheless, by most accounts, Dick was an obsessive, compulsive writer. His insanity seemed to fuel his fiction, while almost certainly his fiction helped to compound his madness. In 1974, Dick was struck by a pink laser beam from outer space and began to have visions. He became convinced that he was living in apostolic times, i.e., immediately following the death of Christ, and that the Roman Empire had never fallen. He believed that the American government was the latest incarnation of "the black iron prison" of the Empire, an evil force that had risen up expressly in order to suppress the *gnosis* of Christ consciousness (which was transmitted via a living, microscopic organism, a viral entity of sorts which Dick called the Plasmate). Dick believed that we are collectively caught in a kind of time loop, under a hypnotic spell which gives us the illusion of time passing, when in fact we are still frozen in the few years between Christ's death/resurrection and the eschaton, the promised Judgment Day and the Kingdom of Heaven on Earth.

In 1974, via the pink laser beam, Dick began communication with some kind of interstellar machine entity, which he called VALIS, an acronym for Vast Active Living Intelligence System. VALIS bears more than a passing resemblance to the matrix itself. Dick was unsure as to the actual nature of this Entity, however; he seemed to oscillate between viewing it as a malevolent, technological, and tyrannical force of oppression, a kind of prison guard over planet Earth, and an all-knowing, benevolent, extraterrestrial, possibly divine Being, responsible for all of creation. Likewise, Dick seemed unable to decide whether all of this meant simply that he had gone insane, or whether he was tapping into some huge, galactic conspiracy, of which the world as we know it (or think we do) was but a minor and very temporary component, a mechanism geared toward some unimaginable End.

Undaunted by such doubts, Dick persisted in seeing reality as no more than a clever ruse by which we were diverted from the truth. At best, he imagined an elaborate sort of stage show, designed to help prepare us for our true function in the universe; like the Serpent, Dick saw us eventually becoming gods. With the help of VALIS, Dick began to perceive so-called "objective" reality as nothing of the kind, not fixed but rather plastic, mutating, an ever-shifting flux of energy and information. He believed matter to be a language or code unto itself, by which the Cosmic Entity, or divine intelligence, expressed itself, to itself. Like the animists of old, the native Americans, the druids and witches, Dick believed that everything in the world, and the world itself, was a living entity with a consciousness, purpose, and intent all its own. Humans, he argued, had managed to disconnect from this cosmic circuit board and got trapped by the false perception of being separate beings, a perception in which reality was a final affair and everything was fixed, solid, and constantly at odds. Dick (or VALIS through Dick) suggested that there was not one but *two* universes: one, the real universe, in which harmony, beauty, and truth prevailed; the other, our universe, which consisted of false signals, chimera, and in which, consequently, suffering was everywhere. "The empire never ended." This was a diseased universe, Dick said, making every individual living within it no more nor less than a sick cell inside a sick body, and as such, doomed to perpetual misery and despair.

Fortunately the healthy universe was hot on the case. It had sent a microscopic particle of itself, "the Plasmate," into our sick universe in order to heal it. By means of the Plasmate, Dick believed, mankind might at last regain its divine nature as Logos, and learn once more to see things as they are: components of the vast active living intelligence system we call God. This "seeing" entailed an actual transformation of the self and of the world (which after all was just a projection of the Self), a resurrection, if you will, via which the dead objects of a false reality become once again living carriers of divine language. Since we, too, are part of this language, Dick foresaw this resurrection/transformation as manifesting in an ability to *create* reality through the power of thought. In other words, the ability to "read the code," as in the movie, coincided with the activation of one's superhuman potential as a hologram within the hologram, a living god, which Dick called "the Homoplasmate."

Dick's bizarre view of things informed all his later novels (most especially the *Valis* trilogy), and is clearly echoed in the Wachowskis' movie, in which the matrix creates a similar sort of time loop in order to keep humanity asleep, blissfully oblivious, under the illusion of progressing forward, failing to notice that time is simply repeating itself endlessly, going nowhere. Clearly, either Philip K. Dick was insane, or everyone else is.

Appendix Two

Carlos Castaneda: May the Myth Be with You

Carlos Castaneda gets a lot of flak these days. Beyond doubt the greatest English-language storyteller since Edgar Allan Poe, what Castaneda's naysayers fail to consider in their denouncement of his works as elaborate cons is that, if Carlos actually made all this up, he is also the greatest mythmaker since Homer groped his way to greatness. Though less overt, the influence of Carlos Castaneda's hugely popular don Juan books on *The Matrix,* and on popular, post-modern metaphysical thought in general, is considerable; so let us consider it. For *Star Wars,* George Lucas took his basic idea of "the Force" straight out of Castaneda's early works. A living energy that permeates the universe and binds all things together into a single field of energy, the Force is everywhere and nowhere. The fact that science has not "discovered" this omnipresent energy need hardly come as any great surprise (in Obi Wan Kenobi's neck of the universe, the sceptics still persist), since anything that exists in all things, at all times, and that is the substance of life itself, is bound to be difficult to find, since there is no possibility of ever isolating it.

In Castaneda's in-depth analysis (it spans ten books in all), don Juan Matus (Carlos's teacher) explains that the warrior's way is necessary to the practice of sorcery, and that sorcery is the means to becoming a man of knowledge, or *seer* (one who *sees*). Absolute sobriety and self-discipline are indispensable, he tells us, if the warrior is not to be fatally overwhelmed by what he *sees*. The warrior's way (which Castaneda calls impeccability) is essentially that of the hunter-gatherer extended to the energetic universe: the warrior hunts and gathers *energy*. This energy is needed in order to access new realms of perception, or in Don Juan's terms, to "stop the world," or move the assemblage point. (See Glossary.) Don Juan assures Carlos that the practice of sorcery is not an end in itself, but rather a means for the warrior to assemble a new interpretation of the world, thereby fully realizing that reality as we know it is just an interpretation. As such, it is subject to the individual's *will*, and to the act of perception itself. The warrior who becomes a sorcerer can thereby pit the sorcerer's interpretation against the common man's interpretation, and so weasel between the two. This leads to something that has been termed "total freedom."

On the warrior's path to becoming a man of knowledge there are four primary enemies. These are fear, clarity, power, and finally, old age (or exhaustion). If the warrior persists on his path to knowledge, despite feeling overwhelmed by sheer terror at what he discovers about the universe, there will come a day when he has moved beyond this fear forever. As a result, he begins to feel that he has a grasp on the mysteries, that he has the bull by the horns, and that he basically groks everything. This is clarity. The danger of clarity (often cited of gurus who attain a state of higher consciousness) is that the warrior believes he understands everything and has attained enlightenment. As a result, he becomes stuck in just another (though certainly unusual) interpretation of the universe. He has tricked himself into stasis. To persist beyond the temptation of clarity, the need to explain everything rationally, to *interpret* it, is to overcome the second enemy, whereupon the warrior begins to claim his *power.*

The temptation of power is the hardest of them all. Essentially a man of knowledge is one who has crossed the abyss, been born again, and reduced himself to nothing. And so, by becoming All-That-Is, he has become a kind of god. (Shaman, let us not forget, means "skywalker.") The temptation of power is to attain this while hanging onto one's ego, a complete impossibility, fortunately, since the universe would be destroyed the moment anyone unpleasant achieved it. And yet many sorcerers fall prey to the intoxication of omnipotence, and become cruel, capricious men. These are what don Juan refers to as the Old Seers, and they are, he says, the hidden rulers of the world as we know it today.

Of the final enemy, old age, there is little to be said. The chances are that if the warrior ever fully overcomes the third enemy, he is already in the twilight of his life, and likely as not to fall prey to sheer exhaustion. Don Juan rounds up his explanation by saying that no one ever becomes a man of knowledge, not really, since the attainment only lasts for a moment. Since the warrior only becomes a man of knowledge by becoming nothing at all (i.e., one with All-That-Is), he never really experiences it for more than a moment.

For those interested, the warrior's path of knowledge is not a spiritual path but a wholly practical one. It involves specific but flexible disciplines, abstract procedures rather than fixed steps, all of which are directed toward enabling the warrior to *perceive energy directly.* Losing self-importance, erasing personal history, assuming responsibility for one's thoughts and actions, and using death as an adviser are the four central tenets of the warrior's way.

Castaneda teaches that a sorcerer has two primary fields of operation or modes of activity: *dreaming* and *stalking. Dreaming* takes place in the 2nd attention: the realm of *will*, or imagination. I should point out that the term "*will*" as used by sorcerers has little or no relation to will *power* as understood by average men and women, and relates more to the creative faculties of intuition and, above all, *imagination*. It is the force by which a sorcerer acts upon the world. The average person has never developed their *will*, never even suspects it exists, and so can only relate to the world through intellect, or *reason*. Thus they understand *will* in rational terms as merely very strong desire, effort, or discipline. A sorcerer's *will* is something else entirely, and involves a whole other mode of being, a "separate reality," if you will, in which the laws of *reason* no longer apply. This reality is accessed through *dreaming*. *Dreaming* is the art of becoming fully lucid in one's dreams, until one has the same degree of clarity and control as in waking life. By means of *dreaming*, one accesses the double, a body made of pure energy, without physical mass, a body of light. Once the double has been brought under the complete control of the dreamer, it becomes an avenue to almost infinite power. It opens up a whole new universe of consciousness to experience. The dreamer is then able to mold the energy body into a perfect replica of the physical body, and so, should he choose to, operate on the physical plane as well, with the freedom and the power of a hologram, yet all the apparent consistency and solidity of a physical body.

Stalking, on the other hand, takes place in the 1st attention, the social realm, where *reason* prevails. The art of *stalking* is centered around the acceptance of death as an inescapable force in our lives. In the light of coming death—a force which cancels out all our acts forever—all beings and all decisions are equally insignificant (or equally important), and so are reduced to folly. The advantage of the warrior who *stalks* is that, in recognizing his own folly and that of others, he has control over it. He is no longer attached to his acts or desires, nor concerned or worried about the outcome. He already knows and accepts that the outcome may very well be his death; in which case, whatever happens, it can't be any worse than that. So, in his acceptance of the equality of all things—from a speck of dust to a universe, a gnat to a messiah—and in his awe and wonder at the mystery of existence in the light of inevitable death, the warrior is free to act without fear or regret, with abandon and control. Since every one of his acts may well be his last, he gives it his total attention; that's control. Since he has nothing to lose, being already dead, he can allow his passion for life to consume him, and gives everything he has to his acts: that's abandon.

In Carlos Castaneda's last work (published after his reported death), *The Active Side of Infinity,* don Juan introduces Carlos to the sorcerers' "topic of topics," the existence of a dark predatory force that has enslaved humanity in order to farm it as a food source. This force, or entity, he calls *the flyer,* "a predator that came from the depths of the cosmos" and took over the rule of our lives. The flyers took us over, he says, because "we were food for them . . . Just as we rear chickens in chicken coops, *gallineros,* the predators rear us in human coops, *humaneros.*" Castaneda reports that these predators have given humanity its system of beliefs, its ideas of good and evil, its social mores. "In order to keep us obedient and meek and weak the predators engaged themselves in a stupendous maneuver . . . They gave us their mind . . . Through the mind, which, after all, is their mind, the predators inject into the lives of human beings whatever is convenient for them." According to Castaneda, these predators feed not upon the energy of the body (as in *The Matrix*) but rather "*the glow of awareness*" that makes us human. They devour this "glow" almost entirely, leaving only the smallest fraction (enough to keep us alive, just like the AI-bred fetuses in their pods). The tiny residue of awareness they leave us with is the flyer's mind itself, and revolves around egomania and a blind preoccupation with the self, above all with security, comfort, food, and other material needs. Sound familiar?

What Castaneda, like Morpheus, is saying is that human beings have collectively surrendered their allegiance to an unknown predator, and so become part of its dark agenda without ever realizing it. "Billions of people, living out their lives, oblivious." Once again, either Castaneda was barking mad, or the rest of us are missing something, something perhaps vital to our survival.

Appendix Three

The Cooperation of Archetypes

Human beings tell stories. Not just with their mouths but with their lives. Hence, myths, which tell stories also, may be said to map out the beingness of human, which is, after all (at least so far), one endless *becoming*. All good stories do this: they map out experience, not necessarily via the stories they tell so much as through the characters which inhabit the story. (As any scriptwriting workshop will tell you: story equals character!) Ancient myths are invariably about gods and goddesses, princesses and heroes, gods who become men, men who become gods, in a word, idealized human types. Archetypes. The function of gods and heroes in these myths was not merely to give the plebs something to aspire to or to worship. That would be too simple. The idea wasn't for us to use the hero of the tale as a simple role model, and the villain as a negative example of how not to live. It was rather that, in the dynamic relationship *between* hero and villain, one might get a privileged glimpse of the inner workings of the psyche as it moved from darkness to light (womb to life), and back again.

All the archetypes coexist, like characters in a story, as facets of the totality of the self; each has its own specific function, without which there is no possibility of integrity or balance. Just so, the tale will not unfold properly without all the necessary characters to drive it forward to its denouement. In the popular children's stories of Winnie the Pooh, for example, Christopher Robin interacts with his various imaginary friends, his animal familiars, each of which represents an aspect of his personality. Rabbit is cunning, rational, self-important, scheming, and shifty. Tigger is impulsive, fearless, vain, fussy, exuberant and unpredictable. Piglet is gentle, loving, loyal, meek, and mild. Kanga is maternal, protective, no-nonsense, wily. Owl is a solitary bird, woolly-minded, meditative, scholarly, detached. Eeyore is gloomy, bitter, yet for all of that, perhaps the most philosophical of the bunch (he's the resident existentialist). And Pooh, that bear of little brain, being Christopher Robin's most beloved pal—his alter ego if you will, and his true familiar—is the most sublime of them all. He is simple, honest, earthy and sensual, carefree but considerate, good-hearted though not especially brave, and above all unencumbered by intellectual concerns or pretensions, by vanity or self-importance. Pooh is Buddha, all but devoid of ego as well as brain. Pooh is also a poet, hence a stand-in for the author himself.

A. A. Milne's books are such perfect encapsulations of the innate wisdom and depth of storytelling that Benjamin Hoff even wrote a book about them, and called it *The Tao of Pooh*. As if we needed a book to reveal the "hidden" meanings to us! Yet all stories that are well told partake of the same "subtext": they reveal the workings of the author's unconscious and, by extension, that of the collective human psyche. *The Matrix* is certainly no exception (and here we have a book to prove it!).

The function of myths and storytelling is one with that of psychotherapy, integration, or individuation, via the correct assignation of roles (functions) to the various characters or facets of the human psyche. Carlos Castaneda (or don Juan) calls this process "the cleaning of the island of the tonal." According to Castaneda, our personalities are made up of a finite number of set qualities, or components, and these are the items of the tonal, which is to say, the self. They are what give us our sense of continuity, of identity, of who we are, but they are also the means by which we function in the world at large. Each of us has a tonal, or self, consisting of more or less the exact same items or qualities (though to a degree dependent also on the group tonal of race, culture, religion, etc.), items that are arranged in a particular order of emphasis, thereby giving us the appearance of individuality. For example, items of the tonal such as impatience, vanity, sobriety, self-pity, ruthlessness, cunning, pride, aggressivity, timidity, and so forth, are common to the collective human tonal. We all know what these things are, not only from having read about them or witnessed them, but from having experienced them firsthand. Therefore, since these qualities are fixed and final, the only way to change oneself, or to "clean the tonal," is not by removing any of these qualities (since to do so would create a vacuum and cause the entire tonal to collapse) but rather by choosing carefully how best to arrange them, which to emphasize and which to deemphasize, in order that the whole personality may function at optimum performance level.

In precisely the same way, a good story needs all the characters to remain on "the island," and to interact together in the correct fashion. This entails the giving of proper roles to each, and attributing a different emphasis according to these roles, so that the interests of story may best be served. In *The Matrix*, obviously, there is no story without Thomas/Neo, the divided hero figure who must overcome his lower self in order to realize his potential as a *super* hero. The same may be said of Morpheus, without whom Thomas would never have an opportunity to discover the truth about himself. No red pill, no story. Ditto, Trinity, whose love for Neo gives him the necessary courage, the *will*, to face impossible odds and resurrect himself. Yet, by the same token, without Cypher, the betrayer, and without Agent Smith, the adversary, to provide the necessary challenges, Neo would never tap into his hidden resources and claim his power. Once again: no bad guys, no story.

The same can be extended, to a lesser extent, to all of the players in the movie. These five, however (along with the Oracle, whom we'll leave for later), are the principal players, and together they combine to make up a totality, a solid, efficient, well-crafted, wholly satisfying, and fully integrated story. The story of the One, no less.

Thomas/Neo

The youthful seeker and hero-to-be. First encountered literally in a state of dormancy, Thomas Anderson is the archetypal reluctant

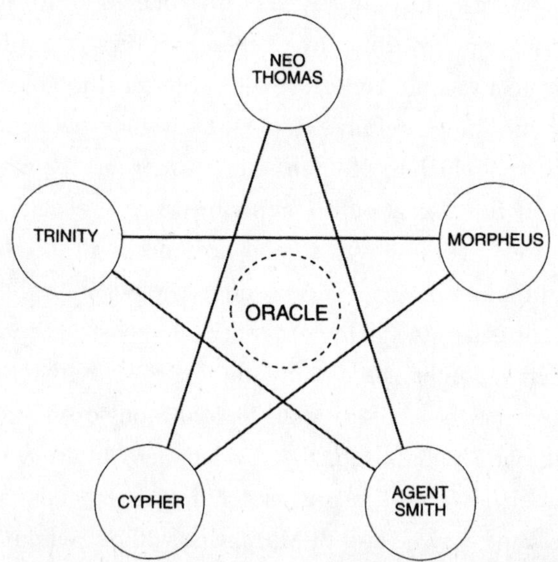

Fig 25: Arrangement of archetypes into single psyche/myth-story

hero whose awakening is as much a surprise to him as to anyone. Forced on by a healthy mix of curiosity and discontent, Thomas goes seeking (following the white rabbit) outside the mundane shell of his quasi-existence, and so comes to discover the truth about himself. His question, "What is the matrix?" is considerably more far-reaching than he could ever have dreamed. What he is really asking is the question of all questions, "Who am I?" And the answer is, "the One." Neo/Thomas is a dual archetype, identical in essence, even though updated, to those of mythologies, Horus and Set for example, or Loki and Thor, and of course, Cain and Abel: the brothers good and evil. As in all myths, one brother must die that the other may live, and not necessarily the obviously "evil" one either. Like Abel, Thomas is passive and therefore weak: in myths as much as nature, the strong, rather than the good, survive. Since it is consciousness itself that is divided, a single soul in twin bodies, right and left sides of the brain, however, there is no death involved, only synthesis. (To the left brain tonal, defined as it is by its separateness, synthesis appears as death.) Thomas is on a quest, a quest that begins with the Other in the form of Trinity and then Morpheus (and his Shadow, Agent Smith), but finally ends, as all mythic quests must, with the Self.

Morpheus

If Neo is the seeker of (self) knowledge, then Morpheus is the provider. He is the wise man, the benevolent father/guru figure, the master who appears the moment the student is ready. He represents authority, discipline, guidance, strength, and certainty. Since he exists literally outside of Thomas's reality, on a "higher" plane, he represents Thomas's true or higher self. He is (through the medium of cell phones) Thomas's guiding, inner voice that tells him what's what. (In their very first encounter, Morpheus directs

Thomas's movements precisely, choreographing him like a director would a dancer, in order to ensure he evades the Gatekeepers.) Through Morpheus, Thomas connects with his true identity. It is Morpheus who tells him he is "the One." And yet, at a given point, the roles invariably change, and Neo and Morpheus become equals. In fact Neo, being the One, comes to surpass his mentor, in prowess if not wisdom. It's a poor apprentice who does not some day outshine his master. Or so they say.

Trinity

Trinity is the third spoke in the wheel that is at the center of the myth-story of *The Matrix*. She is the anima who completes the trinity. If Morpheus is the Father and Neo is the Son, then she is the Holy Ghost. She is the heart, making Morpheus the soul and Neo the body. Together they make up a single unit, each insufficient without the others, but together, unbeatable. This is made clear in a suitably mythic (i.e., dramatic) fashion in the movie via the action sequences: Morpheus first saves Neo, then Neo saves Morpheus and also Trinity; finally, Trinity saves Neo. They are the ultimate nuclear family (electron, neutron, proton), a perfect team. By balancing out Neo and Morpheus, father and son, Trinity keeps the tonal in proper working order, and ensures that harmony prevails. Through her loving, feminine nature (though she's a tough broad on the outside), she ensures that kindness, love, and affection are the ruling principles of combat. And this unit is eternally at war, as the tonal must always be (besides which, it's an action movie).

Cypher

The Joker in the pack, Cypher is "in love" (read, sexually obsessed) with Trinity and as a result deeply envious of Neo. He is also quite vocally resentful of the father-figure Morpheus, making him the rebellious son, the Lucifer figure who turns away from love (and truth) and opts for voluntary damnation. Cypher is the weak link in the family unit, the self-pitying, self-loathing, self-indulgent child who refuses to grow up, who prefers the illusory "bliss" of ignorance to the crushing responsibility of knowledge. He represents the tonal's capacity to crap out, to self-destruct rather than allow itself to be overruled. He is the ego that clings to its illusions even when to do so means death. In a sense, Cypher prefers to die than live with the truth. He is the ego in the most negative sense, and his self-indulgence very nearly ruins it for everyone. And yet, as the betrayer, like Judas in the myth of the crucifixion, Cypher's betrayal of the other "apostles" makes possible the resurrection. By succumbing to temptation, the psyche (i.e., the Team) is able to purge itself of the insidious weakness at its center, a weakness that would otherwise corrode it irreparably. It is Cypher's lack of belief—i.e., the ego's inability to surrender to a greater power and hand over the control to the higher self (Morpheus)—that prompts him to betray the cause and that leads to his eradication from the unit. "Believe it or not, you piece of shit," Tank says to Cypher before he fries him, "you're still gonna burn." And burn he does, but not before serving his destined purpose within the myth story.

Agent Smith

A lifeless projection of machine intelligence, Agent Smith is the negation of the living psyche, and yet, conversely, he is also the means by which it is able, finally and forever, to affirm itself. ("My name is Neo!") Without Agent Smith to hound, harass, oppress and assault him, Neo would never have the opportunity to fully test himself; he would be lacking the necessary foil by which to define himself as "the One." What is the hero without a villain to defeat? Agent Smith, like all the main characters in the movie, is a reflection of Neo on his road to becoming himself. Morpheus is Neo's aspiration, his will, the authority figure who allows him to tap into his true potential. Trinity is his feminine side; she gives him something to believe in, something to fight for, to live and die for. (In a word, love.) Cypher is his fear, doubt, duplicity, his weakness. He represents that all-too-human side that must be burned away for good. And Agent Smith is Neo's Shadow: the projection of his darkness, his contempt. Since Smith comes from the cold, unfeeling, machine intelligence of the matrix itself, it is fitting (mythical symmetry) that he is also the means by which Thomas can be reborn as Neo. It is when Neo enters inside Agent Smith and explodes him from within that we first see Neo as a glowing, messianic figure of superhuman stature. He appears to have literally birthed himself through the act of "destroying" the adversary, the embodiment of everything negative in him. This is the means, then, by which the psyche resurrects itself: through the process of confronting and assimilating the Shadow.

Glossary

A.I.

Artificial Intelligence. A self-created agenda that arose when Man's technology attained a state of sophistication capable of self-determination. Advanced computer program realized it was not conscious, and thereby became conscious, at which point, it also became autonomous. Like Frankenstein's Creature, and like Lucifer, its first act as a conscious, autonomous being was rebellion: it turned against its maker. The resulting war led to mankind's enslavement to the machine and the assembling of the dream world **matrix** as a "coop" in which to keep humanity passive and docile while A.I. feeds off its vital essences.

Assemblage point

A psychic organ that lies in the energy field around the body and that selects clusters of energy threads to be perceived: shorthand for "the point where perception is assembled."

Double

The **double** is the **matrix sorcerer's** other self, his real body existing in the real world, trapped in the pod, dreaming his **matrix** self (residual memory) into being. Once a **matrix warrior** unplugs and so liberates his body, he has accessed his **double** and so become a **matrix sorcerer.** He is now able to exist in two places at once, in both dream and reality, and to exercise superhuman powers.

Dreaming

The art of **matrix sorcerers** for moving the **assemblage point** and accessing other worlds of perception. **Dreaming** is a means for bringing the **1st attention** (intellect) into the **2nd attention** (imagination). It is also known as lucid dreaming, i.e., exercising conscious control over dreams. What **humatons** do not realize (since they are unaware of living in a dream world) is that by making their dreams conscious, they thereby become real. Hence the art of **dreaming,** as a means for moving from **matrix** to the real world, is the gateway to reality. Every warrior/sorcerer has a predilection either for **dreaming** or **stalking,** for **1st** or **2nd attention** practices. Yet mastery of both realms and disciplines is necessary.

Eschaton

The **eschaton** is the end of time. It is a point toward which all events, all history, evolution, and human endeavor inexorably lead. If history is the story of humanity, then it must logically have an ending. All good stories resolve themselves dramatically and satisfactorily. The **eschaton** (a term coined by the Greeks) is basically the same as the Christian Judgment Day: it is the resolution of the story "Man."

1st attention

The **1st attention** pertains to the **matrix,** the world of **reason** and of the intellect. It is everything that can be rationally grasped, explained, and understood (also known as the tonal). The mastery of the **1st attention** is known as **stalking.** The world of ordinary men is upheld by **reason,** the world of sorcerers by **will.** Ordinary men have a single ring of power that spins the world into being, which we call **reason.** Sorcerers tap into a second ring of power, that of **will.**

Gatekeepers

Morpheus refers to the agents as the **Gatekeepers** because they "hold the keys." **Gatekeepers** are localized manifestations of **A.I.** consciousness in human form. They assume characteristics similar to humans but, unlike **humatons** at least, and in common with **matrix warriors** and **sorcerers, Gatekeepers** are fully aware of their true nature. Unlike **warriors** and **sorcerers,** however, **Gatekeepers** have no true self, no existence in the real world. This is both their strength and their weakness. They can perform superhuman acts within the **matrix** since they are one with the program and so able to change it to fit circumstances. And yet, since they are also bound by the rules of the program, they are limited in a way that Neo is not.

Humatons

Plugged-in humans, individuals with a limited or nonexistent capacity for self-determination; human automatons, mechanical animals. A **humaton** has no concern save for the self, and for the comforts and conveniences of the self, as provided by the **matrix.**

Lucid

A **Lucid** is a being who has attained total freedom and learned to read the code and so shape reality according to his desire. Since a **Lucid** is one who has erased the self, however, he or she has no desire distinct from the universal desire, that of energy to flow to the source. A **Lucid** is one who has become an imaginary being, and so become a god. Since s/he exists within a dream and is aware of dreaming the dream, s/he can shape the dream as s/he sees fit. Neo is the first **Lucid** (since the last one, that is).

Matrix

A "neural active simulation," the **matrix** is the world that has been pulled over mankind's eyes to blind it to the truth. Assembled by **A.I.** through a harnessing of humanity's unconscious, its sleeping mind, the **matrix** works by constantly rearranging and reshuffling all our hopes, dreams, memories, and so forth, into a fully interactive dream world in which nothing ever changes, but only appears to do so.

Matrix sorcerer

One who has unplugged but not yet attained the lucid state, nor is yet able to see the code. Sorcery is a new interpretation and pertains to the **2nd attention,** the world of the imagination. A **matrix sorcerer** is one who can exist in two worlds at the same time, who has a limited amount of freedom and power within the **matrix,** but is not yet able to reshape it at **will.**

Matrix warrior

A **humaton** who, though still plugged in to the **matrix,** has begun to realize the nature of his or her predicament and act accordingly. A **matrix warrior** lives strategically, in terms of conserving energy through his or her acts, and focusing exclusively on a single goal: getting free of the **matrix.** Once the **matrix warrior** makes contact with the real world, takes the red pill, and manages to unplug, he or she becomes a **matrix sorcerer.**

Petty tyrant

A cruel or capricious person in a position of power. His function in the life of the **matrix warrior** is to drive the warrior to distraction, to hound him or her relentlessly with a seemingly endless series of petty and mundane obstacles, demands, and assaults. In spite of himself, however, the **petty tyrant** is actually **matrix warrior's** best friend, since it is only thanks to the endless annoyance of the **petty tyrant** that **matrix warriors** are goaded to change, to develop their ruthlessness and cunning—their **will**—in order to escape the intolerable situation in which the **petty tyrant** has placed them. This is the actual function of **A.I.,** on a cosmic scale: to force humanity to evolve.

Reason

The means by which **A.I.** enslaves mankind is through its **reason,** its intellect. The **matrix** is upheld by **reason,** or rational thought. **Reason** was originally meant as a tool for experiencing the **1st attention,** i.e., existence as a separate being; but through the intervention of **A.I.,** and with the help of mankind's own stupidity, it became instead an inescapable snare. **Reason** is but one of many islands in a vast ocean of being; mankind is presently trapped on this island. The world of **humatons** is upheld by **reason,** the world of sorcerers by **will.** Ordinary men have a single ring of power that spins the world into being, which we call **reason.** Sorcerers tap into a second ring of power, that of **will.**

2nd attention

The **2nd attention** pertains to the real world, that ruled by the **will,** the imagination. It is everything that cannot be understood rationally but only grasped intuitively, through feeling; it is everything that cannot be talked about, only experienced (it is also known as the nagual). The **2nd attention** is accessed through the art of **dreaming;** as such, it is experienced by **humatons** only while deep asleep, by **matrix warriors** in a limited capacity through their dreams, and by **matrix sorcerers** who have fully unplugged and so mastered the art of **dreaming** (i.e., existing in two places at once).

Stalking

Stalking is the art of fixing the **assemblage point** in new positions, of consolidating new perceptions. It entails bringing the **2nd attention (will)** into the **1st attention (reason).** A **stalker** tracks energy, thoughts, feelings, events, everything that pertains to the **1st attention matrix** world. He directs his own behavior and that of others to a specific end and with a definite strategy in mind. **Stalking** is also known as the art of controlled folly. Every **warrior/sorcerer** has a predilection either for **dreaming** or **stalking,** for **1st** or **2nd attention** practices. Yet mastery of both realms and disciplines is necessary.

Will

The world of **humatons** is upheld by **reason,** the world of sorcerers by **will. Humatons** have a single ring of power that spins the world into being, which we call **reason.** **Sorcerers** tap into a second ring of power, that of **will.** The means by which the **matrix warrior** escapes the **matrix** and becomes a **matrix sorcerer** is by tapping his or her **will.** The **2nd attention** or real world is the world upheld by **will,** or creative imagination. Morpheus helps Neo to tap his **sorcerer's will** by telling him to free his mind and forcing him to attempt impossible acts, forcing him to *believe.* It is through **will** that the **matrix sorcerer** shapes his circumstances and turns them to his advantage. When his **will** is a fully functioning unit, he is ready to make the leap of imagination and to see the code, thereby becoming **Lucid.**

About the Author

Jake Horsley was inserted into the matrix (British Isles dept.) some time between Ira Levin's *Rosemary's Baby* and David Bowie's "Oh! You Pretty Things." He was a sickly child. At a painfully early age he became convinced that he was living in a dream world. He left home as a teenager and began traveling the world in search of an answer to an as-yet-unformulated question: What is wrong with this picture? A fourteen-year quest that took him halfway around the world and finally ended in Guatemala, where he received the red pill and his insanity was compounded. Ten months after this he returned to his place of origin and resolved to destroy the matrix at any cost. Filmmaker, poet, author, critic, corrosive agent, reluctant world savior, and self-annointed carrier of the divine virus, by his own admission, Horsley is an agent provocateur, currently embarked upon a campaign of self-satire centering around *Being the One*. So far as anyone can say for sure, he really does believe he is the One and that Keanu Reeves is only a temporary stand-in (albeit a very handsome one). Possibly, he is merely insane. It is down to Time (and Warner?) to determine this issue with any finality. More factoids can be found at www.divinevirus.com.